THE SECOND COMING OF JESUS CHRIST

Oil, Terrorism & Nuclear War

DAVID M. TYLER

The Second Coming of Jesus Christ
Oil, Terrorism & Nuclear War
by David M. Tyler, Ph.D.

Scripture references are quoted from
The King James Version of the Bible

Cover design by Melanie Schmidt

ISBN 978-1-885904-92-8

PRINTED IN THE UNITED STATES OF AMERICA
BY
FOCUS PUBLISHING
Bemidji, Minnesota

TABLE OF CONTENTS

INTRODUCTION

On the cornerstone of the United Nations building in New York City is a quotation from the prophet Isaiah:

They shall beat their swords into plowshares, and their spears into pruninghooks: nation shall not lift up sword against nation, neither shall they learn war any more (Isaiah 2:4).

Throughout history mankind has sought after peace. "The war to end all wars" was often associated with President Woodrow Wilson. It was a term used to describe World War I. But it later became apparent the war had not succeeded in ending war, for soon there was World War II.

While there are those who believe that world peace is theoretically possible and war is not an innate part of human nature, peace, nevertheless, eludes mankind. History is a continuous documentation of wars and conflict. Terrorism, "traditional" and nuclear, has created a threat unprecedented in the history of mankind. Leaders race from one part of the globe to another defusing conflict that could very well ignite the next regional or world war.

In 1949, the World Peace Council, based in more than 100 countries, was created as an integral part of the world peace movement. At that time peace curriculum in schools, colleges and universities in the United States and other countries began encouraging young people to consider peace studies as a viable career path. This would set the stage for the future of the peace movement by educating people in methods of incorporating peace in society. In 1981, the United Nations began Peace Day, as a way to celebrate the efforts of people around the world who worked to promote world peace. September 21, 1982 was the first Peace Day celebrated all over the world.

The above quotation from the prophet Isaiah is taken out of its context. As wonderful as it sounds, it speaks of the time when Jesus Christ returns to this earth and restores order as God originally intended it to be.

For nearly 2000 years, the book of Revelation has been a difficult part of the Bible to understand. It is filled with symbolism, and is therefore, very mysterious. It was not until 1948, when the Jews reestablished their home in Israel, beginning the fulfillment of a major prophecy, that men began to understand the symbolic language found in John's Revelation. Israel's return to the Homeland was like a piece to a puzzle that, when fitted in its place, suddenly reveals the picture. The rest of the puzzle fits together more easily and quickly. In the years since 1948 there have been more books and commentaries written about the book of Revelation than at any time. This is prophecy in itself. The prophet Daniel revealed that people would not understand the book until the last days, when the major events prophesied began to happen.

The Apostle John experienced the most breathtaking event any man could ever know. Just think in John's terms for a moment. Here is a man, 2000 years ago, transported by God's divine time machine into a world where technology was so advanced that it would have been unbelievable even to us a hundred years ago. John, familiar with only the primitive weapons of his day, actually witnessed and described what I believe to be a nuclear exchange. He tells of the countries that will be in power along with their allies. He describes in detail the events that lead to the thermonuclear war and the bloody results of what is called the Battle of Armageddon.

One thing God has always done was to inform His own of His future plans. Throughout history, God has inspired men with prophetic capabilities to forecast events hundreds and even thousands of years in advance. The Holy Bible, which contains the prophecies of future events, is the complete revelation of God to man. In the eighteenth verse of the last chapter of Revelation the Apostle John warns mankind that God will bring extreme punishment on those who add to or alter His prophecy.

In spite of God's warning, false prophets have twisted the Word of God to suit themselves. This generation alone has produced more men claiming to be the Messiah than ever before. Jesus Himself, when asked by His disciples what would be the signs of the end of time, said there would be many false teachers and messiahs (Matthew 24).

Today's world is changing at a high rate of speed. Technology has increased in unimaginable proportions. For thousands of years man relied on animals as a means to accomplish work and transportation. In just over a hundred years man has gone from the horse and buggy to primitive automobiles, to passenger planes that fly non-stop half-way around the world and the space shuttle. The phenomenal scientific developments of our age have taken even modern day man by surprise. Alexander Graham Bell's invention of the telephone in 1876 revolutionized communication. Today, Bell's invention has lead to cell phones with global positioning, texting and email capabilities. In 1998 construction in space of the International Space Station (ISS) began, with a completion date in 2012. It is the largest artificial satellite that has ever orbited the earth. It is operated by six astronauts and cosmonauts. The station program has maintained an uninterrupted human presence in space since the launch of Expedition 1 in October 2000.

Technology has amazed us in many ways but none as incredible as the way it has brought the realities of war into our homes via radio and television. On December 8, 1941 President Roosevelt gave what became known as the *Infamy Speech* to a joint session of Congress. The six and a half minute speech was broadcast live by radio and attracted the largest audience in radio history, with over 81 percent of American homes tuning in to hear the President.

In 1965, Vietnam was the first "television war" or "living room war." For years the Saigon bureau was the third largest maintained network after New York and Washington. In 1998, 24 hour news channels held a captivated audience as cameras mounted in aircraft showed "smart bombs" blowing up buildings and bridges in Baghdad, Iraq. More incredible were the miniature cameras on individual bombs or missiles as they traveled to their target. Jacqueline E. Sharkey, in an article written in the *American Journal Review,* entitled *The Television War,* said, "The images that television news crews transmitted to viewers showing the U.S. invasion of Iraq were unprecedented. The networks were able 'to bring this war into the living rooms of Americans.'" Quoting Marcy McGinnis, senior vice president of news coverage for CBS News, Sharkey wrote, "It's the first time you can actually see what's happening." The world can now experience simultaneously the events that are shaping the lives of all mankind.[1]

People are worried about their future. Every day we hear of another impending crisis in one or more parts of the world. Nine nations possess nuclear weapons capabilities while others are racing to join them. The world is held in a fragile balance that could at any moment be shattered by an act of terrorism, failed diplomacy, or a simple accident. What will the future bring? Who can predict it with any accuracy? People today are spending large amounts of money on fortune tellers, soothsayers, and so-called modern day prophets. They subscribe to online and print newspapers and magazines just to read their daily horoscope. People are fearful and nervous about the times in which we live. They feel vulnerable. They are looking for answers.

"Surely I Come Quickly."
Revelation 22:20

---

[1] www.ajr.org/article.asp?id=2988

CHAPTER ONE
The Searching Generation

We've been described as the searching generation,
Looking at our problems with rapt anticipation
Trying to answer questions that plague the whole earth—
Where do we go from here, what's truth, what's worth?

What religion can be trusted when we take our final breath?
What lies in the future? What happens after death?
Is government by the people or of a puppeteer?
Is there a Sovereign Hand to guide this massive swirling sphere?

They say that our dilemma can be cured by education;
More teachers; better schools for a smarter generation.
Our politicians in good faith present their best-made plans,
But fail to find the answers that haunt the minds of man.

Governments change, men falter, ideas are cast aside;
Nothing changed, nothing altered, man and "fate" collide.
Man has searched in other places: science, philosophy,
Meditation, separation; back through history.

But still with all his intellect he's failed to read God's Word,
And when confronted with the text, answers back, "Absurd!"

Is there life after death? Is there really a God? What religion is the right religion? What's going to happen if our present rate of debt keeps growing? Can we trust our political leaders to do what is best for the people and not what is just politically expedient? What about terrorism and the oil crisis? What can we do about the population explosion? According to the television program, *Journey to Planet Earth* (PBS), the earth's population is growing at about 78 million people a year. The United States and other countries produce enough food to feed the world; however, there are a plethora of problems with getting that food to the people—financial, political, and so on. What can we do about the increasing rate of crime and violence related to crimes? Why is suicide the third leading cause of death among teenagers?[2] Questions concerning a multitude of problems and political issues such as debt, unemployment, war, terrorism, crime, and healthcare, are the concern of every nation.

America is no longer secluded from the rest of the world. The miracles of science and technology have made the countries of the world like houses in a subdivision. Their problems are now our problems and our problems are theirs. If there is turmoil among nations we must all enter in and find some means to settle the dispute for fear it might spread into worldwide conflict. We are all in reach of one another.

From the ancient pharaohs who hired and kept a personal staff of astrological advisors, soothsayers, and "prophets," to the rulers and governors of our modern sophisticated society we see the great demands for "seers of the future." It is indeed a strange fact that the most scientifically sophisticated generation of all history is still practicing the ancient Babylonian concepts of the universe fifty centuries later.

The popularity of soothsayers, fortune-tellers and psychics has grown significantly over the last twenty years. According to the *Pew Forum for Religion and Public Life,* one in seven Americans consulted a psychic or fortune-teller in 2009. It's not just the average man or woman either. CEOs of large corporations have sought out the services of fortune-tellers to guide them in personal and business decisions. Throughout American history presidents and politicians have regularly consulted psychics (including George Washington, Abraham Lincoln, Franklin D. Roosevelt, Ronald Reagan, and Woodrow Wilson.)[3]

---

[2]   http://www.teensuicide.us/articles.html

[3]   http://www.psychicreviewonline.com/presidents-that-consulted-psychics.php

America has more than 10,000 professional full-time astrologers, psychics and fortune-tellers, and 175,000 part-time. Americans spend more than $200 million annually consulting these "professionals" to learn what they can about their future. For comparison, there are only about 3,000 astronomers, and approximately $100 million annually, is spent on basic astronomy research. Horoscopes appear in virtually every major newspaper and magazine throughout the United States. The fear of job loss and an unstable economy have boosted the business of hundreds of online fortune-telling websites. The *American Association of Psychics* is a clearing house for psychics, mediums, astrologers, numerologists, and spiritual coaches. Their slogan is "Light Workers Around the World Unite: We Too Can Make a Difference." They refer to themselves as "light workers," spreading light, enlightening people, and guiding them in truth.

Rosemary, "The Celtic Lady" ™, world-renowned psychic, medium, medical intuitive, member of the *American Association of Psychics*, and CEO and Founder of the *American, Canadian, and UK Associations of Psychics and Healers* said, "I have been receiving messages from Joshua my spirit guide as far back as I can remember. For years now he has been pressing me to bring all the Light Workers together from all over the world …"[4] The *Lifetime* television network presents a reality competition program called *America's Psychic Challenge* that features sixteen contestants who claim to have the gift of clairvoyance. In each episode, participants must prove their psychic abilities through a series of tests. The competitors are awarded points based on the accuracy of their predictions. At the conclusion of each episode, the two psychics with the fewest points are eliminated. The two with the most points will advance to the next round. The season finale will be when one winner is declared to be "America's Number One Psychic." *Art and Entertainment* Television's *Psychic Kids: Children of the Paranormal* profiles the lives and experiences of children who have psychic abilities.

---

[4]   http://www.americanassociationofpsychics.com/Mission_Statement.php

The prices for a psychic reading over the phone may vary from one to five dollars per minute. Some celebrity psychics charge their clients seven hundred dollars or more for a psychic reading lasting around 20 minutes.[1] Reputable astrologers are sometimes kept on a retainer ($400 to $500 per month) by wealthier clients, allowing those clients to call anytime, and anywhere, for a consultation.

There's Profit in Being a Prophet

Presidents, students, husbands and wives
Confide in their prophets and wizards.
Seers and astrologers look to the skies
For the bull, the lion, and lizard.

An obsession to learn what the future holds
Is as common as apple pie.
And in an attempt to learn what's to come
They look for signs in the sky.

Astrology books by the dozens
Sell as fast as they're put on the rack.
So popular stores just can't keep up
They're printed in mass paperback.

Selling better than papers and magazines
Instead of those bold headlines
Telling of earthquakes, famine and war,
And horrid perverted crimes.

The future is big business
Foretelling it in such demand
That millions of dollars each year
Are passed to the soothsayer's hand.

Yes, the future is indeed a serious and profitable business. Colleges and universities across the country have become astrology-minded, offering classes in astrology and witchcraft. Department stores across the nation offer everything from zodiac cocktail glasses and paper napkins to personalized T-shirts with the twelve signs of the zodiac. And like everything else, astrology has become computerized. Astrology software can save and retrieve an individual's data, compare the planet positions of different charts, generate colorful maps and provide interpretive text into a narrative report.

How can we know who has been inspired by God in a generation where we are constantly bombarded by these self-acclaimed seers, fortune-tellers and "prophets of truth"? The Koran identifies a number of men as "Prophets of Islam." Muhammad is the last of the prophets, sent for the whole of humankind. Joseph Smith, of the *Church of Jesus Christ of Latter-Day Saints*, established in 1830, is considered a prophet by members of the LDS church. The Seventh-Day Adventist Church, established in 1863, believes Ellen G. White, one of the church's founders, was given the spiritual gift of prophecy. Michel de Nostradamus was a French apothecary and reputed seer who published collections of prophecies that have since become famous worldwide. Are all of these people prophets sent from God? Are there certain standards that God's prophets must live up to before they can be considered real and genuine? The answer to this question is yes; there are standards which a true prophet must meet, so we can recognize him from the impostors.

The warning against false prophets and teachers is echoed throughout the Old and New Testaments. We hear the Psalmist telling of his experience with false teachers (Psalm 27:12). In the *Sermon on the Mount,* Jesus spoke to a multitude of people, warning them against false prophets who come disguised as humble servants, when in reality they are untrustworthy and dangerous as wolves. On the Mount of Oiives, Jesus told His disciples:

> **Take heed that no man deceive you. For many shall come in my name, saying I am Christ; and shall deceive many** (Matthew 24:4, 5).

And many false prophets shall arise, and shall deceive many. For there shall arise false Christs, and false prophets, and shall show great signs and wonders; insomuch that, if it were possible, they shall deceive the very elect (Matthew 24:11, 24).

I remember a school teacher once saying that if something was worth repeating, it was worth remembering. And sure enough, at a test or final examination you would find questions on those things that were emphasized by discussion or repetition. Jesus was on earth for only a short time so He had to make every day count. His main goal was to reveal Himself as the long-awaited Messiah, atoning for the sin of mankind, and teach His chosen disciples how to carry on His teachings after He had gone. Therefore, everything Jesus said He said because it was important. And by the same token, everything He repeated we can assume was of the utmost importance.

Jesus describes a false prophet as wearing sheep's clothing, **"Beware of the false prophets, which come to you in sheep's clothing, but inwardly they are ravening wolves"** (Matthew 7:15). The term "sheep's clothing" emphasizes the danger of false prophets. Outwardly, they appear harmless. They disguise themselves and are extremely subtle. They look all right. Nobody suspects anything. The false prophet is an individual who comes in with all the appearance of being a believer. He is nice and he seems to say all the right things. His teachings in general seem fine. He uses many of the terms that Christians use. He talks about God, Jesus, and the cross. There is nothing about his language or behavior that arouses your suspicion.

Anyone can detect an individual whose behaviors and words are shamefully wrong and sinful. Error is obvious to Christians when they hear things that are blatantly wrong. But they have difficulty distinguishing error when a person seems to say all the right things but leaves out *vital* things. The most dangerous person of all is the one who does not emphasize the *right* things.

The false prophet disguises himself, and so there is nothing blatantly wrong or offensive about him. He pleases everyone. His message is nice, comfortable and pleasing to men. He is all things to all men. The false teacher is always comforting. As you listen to his message you get the impression that everything is fine and nothing is wrong. He fits the description of the false teachers in Jeremiah's day who said, "Peace, peace," when there was no peace. To the false prophet, Jeremiah was narrow-minded, harsh and unloving. The false prophet is always emphasizing the positive aspects of humanity.

Jeremiah lamented how the false prophets and teachers of Israel had not taken God's warnings of judgment seriously. God warned them on numerous occasions that their disobedience would lead to severe consequences. Sadly, the false teachers minimized God's words by giving a false impression to the nation that all was well. They comforted the people, making them happy, but their words were untrue. Jeremiah said, **"They have healed also the hurt of the daughter of my people slightly, saying, 'Peace, peace'; when there is no peace"** (Jeremiah 6:14).

German philosopher George W. F. Hegel (1770-1831) said, "History teaches us that history teaches us nothing." In the past seventy years we have witnessed two World Wars, the Korean War, Vietnam War, Iraq War, dozens of other skirmishes, the destruction of the World Trade Center and so on. In spite of all that we have experienced, mankind continues to embrace the same fatal optimism about humanity as the prophets in Jeremiah's day. The true prophets warned them that unless they repented the consequences would be harsh and exacting. The false teachers, however, told them things were not as bad as Jeremiah was telling them. They assured the people that everything would be fine and told them not to worry. God's true prophets, like Jeremiah, were loathed because of their message. The false prophets were loved, but were ultimately proven to be wrong. God's patience had run its course and judgment came upon Israel.

I recently read an interview with Valerie Morrison, an internationally acclaimed psychic from Philadelphia. She states that her prophetic abilities come from God, but she admits that she is not infallible and claims an accuracy of 85 percent. Would God give one of His own prophets false and misleading information fifteen percent of the time? Of course not! Therefore, according to the Bible, Valerie Morrison is not a prophet sent from God.[5]

While browsing in my local bookstore, I found a copy of a book by Ruth Montgomery entitled, *A Gift of Prophecy: The Phenomenal Jean Dixon*. As I opened the cover I read a list of her predictions, one being: "Russia will be the first nation to put men on the moon." Needless to say, she was wrong. Granted, Jean Dixon and others have made some amazing predictions that have come true. This writer is convinced that anyone can make predictions with a certain degree of accuracy. But to prophecy hundreds and even thousands of years in advance with pinpoint accuracy time and time again is a test that only God's prophets can pass. And remember, a prophet of God's must be 100 percent accurate.

When a prophet speaketh in the name of the LORD, if the thing follow not, nor come to pass, that is the thing which the LORD hath not spoken, but the prophet hath spoken it presumptuously: thou shalt not be afraid of him (Deuteronomy 18:22).

We must evaluate a prophet not by our standards, but by God's standard.

A True Prophet

How will we know a true prophet?
When there are hundreds that profess
To have insight from God, the Father,
And are favored and miraculously blessed?

5   http://www.themetaarts.com/archives/200301/valeriemorrisonint.html

How shall we live in this turmoil?
Our heads spinning round and round
To keep the cults and the mystics,
From running our faith-boat aground.

But our Captain, knowing we falter,
Has prepared things He knew we would ask,
By calming the seas when they're stormy,
With Scriptures that teach and relax.

Would these prophets today stake their lives?
On the claims they insist are divine?
With no margin of error to save them,
Would they risk their lives or decline?

The lives of the prophets of Israel
Were dependent on visions they told,
Could these prophets today be as certain,
As faithful, confident, and bold?

Would I be presumptuous in saying
That none could make such a claim?
For even Jean Dixon admitted herself
That she'd not always had perfect aim.

Then how may we know a true prophet
From someone that we may suspect?
How accurate are their prophecies?
God's prophets are always correct.

CHAPTER TWO
One Messiah, Two Comings

The central theme of the Jewish prophets was that of the coming Messiah, and how He would fulfill the promises God had made to their forefathers. The ironic thing about it is that when Jesus came, the majority of the religious leaders of that day did not recognize Him as the long-awaited Messiah. Why?

The Old Testament prophets gave two descriptions of the coming Messiah. One described the Messiah as a mighty, conquering king who would come down at the height of a global war and save the Jewish people from their enemies. He would be a political Messiah and would rule over the entire earth. The other described the coming Messiah as a humble servant who would suffer for others and be rejected by His own people. This is just the opposite of the previous description and, understandably, the less popular of the two.

This was difficult for the rabbis to understand, and therefore, they theorized that there would be two Messiahs. The rabbis refused to accept the idea that the two descriptions were actually of the same Person. It would be like looking at a range of mountains. You see the top of one mountain and beyond it the summit of a second. From your perspective you cannot see the beautiful valley that separates the two mountains. Men viewed the two portraits of the Messiah in the same manner. They saw two different persons, but missed the connection. They did not understand the two roles of the Messiah, one a sufferer and the other a deliverer, and how they would be separated by a valley of time.

From our present-day vantage point, we clearly understand that instead of having two Messiahs we have one Messiah with two comings and two roles separated by 2,000 years. The prophet Daniel foretold that when the Messiah comes the first time He will be **"cut off, but not for himself …"** (Daniel 9:26). The Messiah would die for others, not because of any guilt or sin in Himself. His first coming, following His death and burial, demands a resurrection and ascension into heaven in order for there to be a second coming. Jesus Christ's second coming will occur at the end of the world (Matthew. 24:3).

Jesus of Nazareth was not accepted by the Jews as their Messiah. But the prophecies concerning the birth, ministry, miracles, death, resurrection, and the fact that He would not be accepted as the Messiah, all coincide with the life of Jesus. Is this coincidence? If so, why hasn't the human race produced another man like Him? Could hundreds of prophecies have been made and coincidently fulfilled by anyone?

We find over 300 prophecies in the Old Testament concerning the coming Messiah that were discounted by the Jewish people (See Appendix 1). These prophecies were fulfilled to the letter by a carpenter's son named Jesus. They are historical events that have molded and shaped the world in which we live.

Out of the hundreds of prophecies the Bible records for us, nearly all but a handful have been literally fulfilled. Today's world events are at this very minute shaping the world for the dynamic conclusion of the prophecies found in God's Word. But will we listen? If a fortune-teller today with an accuracy rate of 85 percent speaks, his or her predictions make headlines in the newspaper. Everyone perks up and listens to this great "prophet" because of their outstanding degree of accuracy. Yet it is distressing that the prophets of God have been ignored by our "searching generation."

There are many predictions that repeatedly warn us of the return of Jesus Christ. The only reason mankind today is unaware that most of the prophecies have been fulfilled is because we are ignorant of the prophecies in the first place. Major political decisions of this generation were prophesied 2000 years ago by Jesus Himself. The rise of Russia and China to world prominence was predicted thousands of years ago by the prophet Daniel. The Arab-Israeli conflict was also predicted by biblical prophets. And if you've ever wondered about the possibilities of a nuclear war, the Apostle John gives us a vivid description in the book of Revelation. Yes, Jesus is going to return, but this time, instead of a humble Messiah, He will be a reigning Messiah, bringing judgment down upon those who have rejected and opposed Him.

The phenomenon of fulfilled prophecy is strong evidence of biblical inspiration. The Bible is a unique book among religious books. Other books may contain vague predictions, but there is nothing comparable to the Bible. The so-called modern prophets, such as Nostradamus, Jean Dixon and so on, have made many predictions. However, their prophecies are ambiguous and can be interpreted in a variety ways. Some appear to have come to pass in a general way, but most of their predictions have failed.

A legitimate prophet, a prophet sent from God, can stand the test of time. A prophet's predictions must predate the event, must be specific and not vague, and must be beyond man's ability to calculate and manipulate. The prophecy must be something that man could not do without God's divine intervention. Only God Himself knows the future. Only God can **"calleth those things which be not as though they were"** (Romans 4:17). Only God is capable of **"Declaring the end from the beginning, and from ancient times the things that are not yet done …"** (Isaiah 46:10).

If a person can demonstrate the ability to predict future events with exact precision and fulfillment then that person is speaking on behalf of God. He must be 100% accurate.

Most of the three hundred plus prophecies found in the Old Testament concerning the Messiah were written over a period of one thousand years and beyond the control of any man. For example, concerning Jesus' birth (the place, time and manner), death (people's reactions, the piercing of His side, and burial), and resurrection (where did His body go) were all recorded in different places in Scripture.. Every prediction was exactly fulfilled in Jesus Christ, thus confirming His credentials as the Messiah.

The mathematical probability of one person fulfilling just eight of any of the prophecies concerning Jesus Christ would be one in one hundred trillion. To illustrate the enormous chance of Jesus Christ fulfilling eight prophecies if He was not the Son of God, imagine one hundred trillion silver dollars spread across the state of Texas, (one hundred trillion silver dollars would cover the state two feet deep), with one of those silver dollars marked with a black X. For Jesus to have accidently or coincidently fulfilled eight of those prophecies would be like a blindfolded man finding that one silver dollar on his first attempt.[6]

Jesus fulfilled over three hundred prophecies written about the Messiah. That was only possible because the prophets were God's prophets and Jesus was the Son of God.

---

[6]   http://home.surewest.net/dfrench/evidence/prophecy.htm

CHAPTER THREE
The Key to the Prophetic Puzzle

"A puzzle tests our wit,"
A poet once had writ,
But never would admit
He sometimes threw a fit.

From his desk he would flee
From great catastrophe.
To the ceiling he would plea,
"Oh, help me find the key!"

For hours he would try
Until he thought he'd die.
"I need the piece whereby
The answer will supply."

All night he vowed to work
Till his head began to jerk.
Then with a sudden smirk,
His back began to perk.

"I found the piece I need!"
Confirmed it with "Indeed!"
Then rubbed his hands in greed.
The answer came with speed.

The key to the puzzle,
The Bible gives the clue,
We should have known it long ago,
The answer is the Jew.

About 3700 years ago God came to a man called Abraham. Up until this time God had revealed Himself to all mankind but man continually ignored Him and lived in every kind of sin. God had already destroyed the earth by water because of man's wickedness. Later, in Genesis, chapter 11, He confounded man's language, scattering people to all parts of the world. Man still paid no attention to God. Therefore God revealed Himself in a special way to Abraham, promising him that if he would obey His commands, God would bless his descendants, making them a great nation. Abraham trusted God and followed His command.

I will bless thee, and in multiplying I will multiply thy seed as the stars of the heaven, and as the sand which is upon the sea shore ... And in thy seed shall all the nations of the earth be blessed; because thou hast obeyed my voice (Genesis 22:17,18).

God's purpose in choosing the Jewish race was for it to serve God in a very special way. It would be through Abraham's descendants that God would send the Messiah. Every book of the Old and New Testaments was written by a Jewish writer. It was the Jewish people who protected and preserved the early manuscripts of the Bible. Isaiah's manuscript was discovered among the *Dead Sea Scrolls* in the late 1940s. It was approximately 2200 years old when it was compared to the manuscript which we know today; the manuscripts were identical.

Moses' Great Prophecy

Of all the Jews, Moses is perhaps one of the most revered. He was a man whom God had selected for a special task. Moses would be used by God to deliver His people from Egyptian slavery. He was also a prophet, and as Moses led the Israelites out of their captivity and into the land promised by God to their forefathers, he made some astounding predictions concerning their future. Five chapters in the book of Deuteronomy are devoted to the blessings for their obedience and the curses for their disobedience to God.

The Lord shall send upon thee cursing, vexation, and rebuke, in all that thou settest thine hand unto for to do, until thou be destroyed, and until thou perish quickly; because of the wickedness of thy doings, whereby thou hast forsaken me. The Lord shall cause thee to be smitten before thine enemies: … and shalt be removed into all the kingdoms of the earth (Deuteronomy 28:20, 25).

As predicted, Abraham's descendants broke the covenant that they originally made with God. Years later, because of their idol worship and sin, God sent a curse upon the Israelites and they were carried off for 70 years to serve the Babylonian nation as slaves. At the end of these 70 years, they were released by King Cyrus, who had been predicted by name 200 years before by the prophet Isaiah.

They were again subjected to God's curse as predicted by the prophets Isaiah, Jeremiah, and Amos, when they rejected God's only Son. And before His arrest, Jesus Himself told of the great distress that would begin with that generation. It was less than 40 years later that Roman legions destroyed Jerusalem, fulfilling His prophecy.

So instead of continuing to bless Abraham's descendants, God cursed their nation, and scattered them all over the world.

> Israel, O Israel, you're dragged away as slaves,
> Tortured inhumanely, then cast in massive graves.
> As Moses had predicted enroute to the Promised Land,
> For your rejection of the Lord,
> you'll be smitten with an iron hand,
>
> Destroyed as a nation, scattered far and wide,
> Persecuted relentlessly, tortured, crucified.
> Israel, O Israel, you've fallen to your knees,
> Crawled through every nation to find no bit of ease.

Subjected to their will and whatever they request,
With a failing eye and trembling heart,
you'll never be at rest.
Your mind will hang in doubt
with no assurance of your life,
And you'll march to every tune played with the fifer's fife.

Your carcass shall be meat unto the fowls of the air,
The tyrants of the world shall strip your bodies bare.
And for centuries you'll wander as you try to understand
Why your enemies grow prosperous
in your Father's Promised Land.

God's Curse: Even in the Twentieth Century

The Massacre of the Jews:

> There are some things so horrible that decent men and
> women find them impossible to believe, so monstrous
> that the civilized world recoils incredulous before them.
> The recent reports of the systematic extermination of
> the Jews in Nazi Europe are of this order. The program
> is already far advanced. According to the report to the
> President by leaders of American Jewish groups, nearly
> 2,000,000 European Jews have already been slain since
> the war began, and the remaining 5,000,000 now living
> under Nazi control are scheduled to be destroyed as
> soon as Hitler's blood butchers can get around to them.
> (The New Republic, 21 December 1942)

The most recent massive persecution of the Hebrew race took
place in the 1940s when, under the orders of Adolph Hitler, Adolph
Eichmann burst forth in a demonic frenzy, vowing to exterminate the
Jewish population. Only by seeing films of the insides of gas chambers
and listening to eyewitness reports of Nazi soldiers tossing babies into

the air and catching them on their bayonets has mankind had some grasp of the persecution of the Jewish people. Lullabies were played over loudspeakers while children were marched off to gas chambers as their parents watched. Prisoners were used as guinea pigs for "scientific" experiments. Soldiers delighted themselves and practiced their marksmanship by shooting off the fingers, ears, and noses of Jews standing helplessly in huge ditches.

It is hard to believe that a race of people could survive such persecution for more than 2000 years and still exist. I'm sure many of them experienced moments of despair in spite of the future that God revealed through His prophets. It seems that the hopelessness alone would have driven them to extinction.

In Deuteronomy, Moses said that the Jewish people would be "a sign," or an example, to the rest of the world to heed the prophecies of the Lord and that God means what He says and says what He means.

> **And it shall come to pass, when all these things are come upon thee, the blessings and the curse, which I have set before thee, and thou shalt call them to mind among all the nations, whither the Lord thy God hath driven thee … That then the Lord thy God will return and gather thee from all the nations, whither the Lord thy God hath scattered thee. And the Lord thy God will bring thee into the land which thy fathers possessed, and thou shalt possess it …** (Deuteronomy 30:1, 3, 5).

> Oh, Israel,
> You shall possess the land again,
> And Jerusalem will be won;
> Just as the fig tree blooms in spring,
> And east brings up the sun.

Just as the tender branch foretells
That winter's passed away;
And spring has sprung upon us,
And night soon turns to day.

No matter what the odds will be,
Your victories will be great;
As prophesized 2000 years ago,
Fulfilled—May, 1948!

Up until May, 1948, men regarded the prophecies of the book of Revelation as something yet to be fulfilled in some century far off in the future. Preachers and ministers understandably avoided the subject because there was simply nothing to indicate its relevance to present day congregations. After all, the main prophecy concerning the second coming of Jesus Christ had not even taken place.

In Matthew 24, Jesus tells His disciples of some specific events that will be present in the last days before His return. Given that all of these prophecies concern the Jewish people within their homeland of Israel, it is necessary that they be reestablished in that land given to Abraham by God. It is at this point that Jesus describes an invasion of the new state of Israel. This invasion marks the beginning of the final days before a great worldwide conflict that ultimately ends with the physical return of Jesus Christ. In Matthew 24:15 we see another clue to the repossession of Israel by the Jewish people:

When ye therefore shall see the abomination of desolation, spoken of by Daniel the prophet, stand in the holy place ...

Previously, we discussed the prophecy wherein Moses said that for their disbelief in God's Son, the Jewish people would again be scattered to all parts of the world. This prophecy came true in 70 A.D. when the Roman legions destroyed Jerusalem.

In destroying Jerusalem, they destroyed the temple on Mount Moriah, wherein, according to the Law of Moses, the high priest offered sacrifices unto God for the sins of the Jewish people. The "abomination of desolation" is a term used by the Jews which means to desecrate the temple by bringing a Gentile or an unholy thing in it. This happened in 165 B.C. when an invading king entered the temple, set up an idol and slaughtered a pig on the altar. According to the prophecy, the desecration of the temple will be repeated. Paul describes this event:

That man of sin be revealed [antichrist], the son of perdition: Who opposeth and exalteth himself above all that is called God, or that is worshipped; so that he as God sitteth in the temple of God, showing himself that he is God (2 Thessalonians 2:3, 4, parenthesis mine).

The antichrist (a political figure which we will discuss later) will enter the sacred temple and claim to be God. And according to the prophet Daniel, all sacrifices and thanksgiving to God shall cease.

There are other clues to the possession of Israel and Jerusalem before Christ's return when Jesus speaks of the Jewish people fleeing from a great battle into the Judean Mountains. In Matthew 24:20 we see that the ancient tradition concerning traveling on the Sabbath is again enforced. Most importantly, all of this cannot occur until the temple that was destroyed by Titus 2000 years ago is rebuilt. Today, Israel is planning for reconstruction of the place of worship.

The Temple Institute in Jerusalem is dedicated to Israel's rebuilding of the Temple. According to reports, "They could start building tomorrow … They've chosen the location, a computer registry of 300,000 of the sons of Aaron (the Levites), many robes are prepared, over 150 sacred vessels have already been restored … the Menorah and the precious stones of the High Priest's breastplate are also ready."[7]

---

[7]   http://www.templeinstitute.org/main.htm

On February 4, 2011, the Temple Institute released its Temple plans:

Now Presenting the Greatest Progress toward the Rebuilding of the Holy Temple in Modern History:

Blueprints for The Holy Temple. In his recent USA speaking engagement tour, (January 2011), Rabbi Chaim Richman of the Temple Institute revealed to the public for the very first time detailed construction plans for the Chamber of Hewn Stone: the seat of the Great Sanhedrin which is a central component of the Holy Temple complex on the Temple Mount. These complete and highly intricate plans constitute the first stage of an historical undertaking of the Temple Institute: the drafting of blueprints for the entire Holy Temple complex.[8]

One important question must be addressed pertaining to the rebuilding of the Temple, and that is the location. Will the Temple, as many believe, be constructed in the center of the Temple Mount? If so, the Dome of the Rock (the Islamic mosque considered to be the third holiest place in all of Islam) must be torn down. That is unlikely. However, many believe the Temple did not stand in the center of the Temple Mount. There are other theories of where the Temple was once located:

1. Where the *Dome of the Rock* is now located (Dr. Leen Ritmeyer, and Dr. Dan Bahat, archaeological architects of the Temple Mount excavations).
2. Located a little to the north of the *Dome of the Rock* (Professor Asher Kaufman, faculty member in physics at Hebrew University).

---

[8]   http://www.cogwriter.com/news/religious-news/temple-institute-released-tem-ple-plans/

3. Located a little to the east of the *Dome of the Rock* (Professor Joseph Patrich, faculty member at Hebrew University).
4. 110 yards to the south of the *Dome of the Rock* (Grant Jeffrey, Internationally known author and Tuvia Sagiv, Tel Aviv architect).[9]

According to evangelist and author Hal Lindsey, the new temple could be constructed next to the *Dome of the Rock*. Lindsey subscribes to the theory that the *Dome of the Rock* was built on what the Bible refers to as the *Court of the Gentiles*. According to the Apostle John, the building of the new Temple was not to include the section known as the *Court of the Gentiles* (Revelation 11:1, 2). Based on this idea the Jewish Temple could stand beside the *Dome of the Rock*.[10] Construction could start anytime.

The Indestructible Jew

Depending on how one defines a civilization, historians agree that there have been about forty civilizations in the history of mankind. The life spans of these civilizations, as individual subsistent cultures, have been from about 500 to 1000 years. After that a civilization usually becomes stagnant or disintegrates altogether. I am not speaking about survival in a biological sense, since, for example, the Egyptians and Greeks are still moving right along after thousands of years. Instead, I mean a civilization that has been unbroken in the ideas that caused it to evolve in the first place—its culture. When the continuity of those ideas is disrupted, the culture or civilization dies.

An example of a broken society is the Greek Empire. The Greeks of today are not characterized by the same culture as were Greeks in the empire of thousands of years ago. The same can be said of Egyptian culture today as compared to that during the reigning of the pharaohs. No society has been able to survive intact from its beginning. A conquered society will eventually fade and disappear into

[9] http://www.templeinstitute.org/main.htm
[10] Ibid.

a meaningless existence. A culture in exile will ultimately die for lack of identification, as their people integrate into a new society. This is the rule, according to past history; but there is one exception to that rule—the Jews.

The Jews first appeared during the Babylonian Empire, about 2000 B.C. When the Babylonian Empire fell and eventually disintegrated, the Jews appeared in the Persian world. After the Persian Empire fell during the 6th century, the Jews sprouted up in the Hellenic civilization around the late eighth century B.C. Then Rome conquered the world, and with Rome came the Jews.

Although Jewish culture has been present during the decline and fall of every major world civilization, this remarkable race has always popped right back up, unbroken, in the midst of another era. While other great world powers have come and gone, the Jews have been preserved as a distinct and separate nationality. In spite of tremendous odds against their continuity, historians have traced them back nearly 4000 years to Abraham.

Why the Jews? The answer to that question, quite simply, is God's covenant with Abraham. God, unlike man, keeps and honors His promises—something for which we should all be grateful. Throughout Jewish history we see a people who have been preserved and given the miraculous ability to survive, even when confronted by innumerable obstacles.

> The phenomenal survival of the Jewish population
> Mysteriously presents a prophetic education.
>
> Contradicting natural law that a people could exist
> As sympathetic victims of horrendous prejudice,
>
> Jewish survival—what word would best define
> This miracle of history other than divine?

Just as the Jews once hoped for the day when they could return to their homes in the land promised to them by God, so the Arabs today cling to the hope of driving Israel into the Mediterranean and claiming the entire land, including the city of Jerusalem. Because of its superior size, number of people, and increasing wealth due to vast oil deposits, the Arab world is convinced today that achieving this goal is only a matter of time. Yes, it is prophecy that the Middle East will be the major hot-spot threatening world peace.

In the past 100 years we have seen the promises of God to the Jewish people come to fruition. After World War I, the British government, under the direction of Arthur Balfour determined that the Jews should have a homeland forever. On November 2, 1917, The Balfour Declaration was signed. This formal document stated that His Majesty's government views with favour the establishment in Palestine of a national home for the Jewish people, and will use their best endeavours to facilitate the achievement of this object, it being clearly understood that nothing shall be done which may prejudice the civil and religious rights of existing non-Jewish communities in Palestine, or the rights and political status enjoyed by Jews in any other country.[11]

The anniversary of this declaration is widely commemorated in Israel and among Jews as Balfour Day. This day is also observed as a day of mourning and protest in Arab countries.[12]

After World War II, when the free world learned of the devastation of the Jews in the holocaust, there was global agreement that the Jews should have a homeland. Finally, on May 14, 1948 in Tel Aviv, Jewish Chairman David Ben-Gurion proclaimed officially the State of Israel, establishing the first Jewish state in 2000 years. He later became Israel's first prime minister.

In the distance, the rumble of guns could be heard from fighting that broke out between Jews and Arabs imme-

---

[11] www.wikipedia.org/wiki/Balfour_Declaration_of_1917#cite_note-0
[12] Ibid.

diately following the British army withdrawal earlier that day. Egypt launched an air assault against Israel that evening. Despite a blackout in Tel Aviv—and the expected Arab invasion—Jews joyously celebrated the birth of their new nation, especially after word was received that the United States had recognized the Jewish state. At midnight, the State of Israel officially came into being upon termination of the British mandate in Palestine.[13]

In the United States, President Harry Truman made the decision to recognize the establishment of the State of Israel over the objections of Secretary of State George Marshall, who feared it would hurt relations with the Arab states. At a meeting in the White House on November 10, 1945, he told envoys to Saudi Arabia, Syria, Lebanon and Egypt: "I am sorry, gentlemen, but I have to answer to hundreds of thousands who are anxious for the success of Zionism: I do not have hundreds of thousands of Arabs among my constituents."[14]

Ultimately, Truman and Congress continued to support the establishment of a homeland for the Jewish people. In his memoirs, Truman wrote that top Jewish leaders in the United States put pressure on him to promote Jewish aspirations in Palestine. Truman recognized the State of Israel on May 14, 1948, eleven minutes after it declared itself a nation.[15]

Truman wrote:

> Hitler had been murdering Jews right and left. I saw it, and I dream about it even to this day. The Jews needed

---

[13] Ibid.

[14] Harry S. Truman, *Memoirs 2*, p. 153.

[15] Truman, Harry (May 14, 1948). "Memo recognizing the state of Israel". Truman Presidential Museum & Library. Retrieved April 2, 2007.

some place where they could go. It is my attitude that the American government couldn't stand idly by while the victims [of] Hitler's madness are not allowed to build new lives.[16]

In October, 1956, Israel easily overran that portion of land known as the Gaza Strip. If they had not been stopped by the major world powers, Egypt would have easily fallen to the Israelis. Years later, Egypt moved into a closer alliance with Russia, who began supplying them with military advisors and weapons. The Unites States countered their move by aiding Israel with arms.

In 1967, Egypt's President Nasser decided it was time to destroy Israel. Nasser's goal was to destroy every Jew that breathed, thus claiming the land for Egypt. This war lasted only six days. The Egyptian losses were devastating. Instead of exterminating the Jews, the Arab forces themselves were demolished. Nasser's dream was shattered. Again prophecy was fulfilled; as a result of the six-day blitz, the Jews had conquered the city of Jerusalem.

For hundreds of years, critics of the Bible have laughed at the promises that God made to Abraham and his descendants. Even in the face of such constant harassment the Jew has clung tenaciously to the promises of God. Today the scoffers have been silenced by the fulfillment of these promises:

> **And I will bring again the captivity of my people of Israel, and they shall build the waste cities, and inhabit them; and they shall plant vineyards, and drink the wine thereof; they shall also make gardens, and eat the fruit of them. And I will plant them upon their land, and they shall no more be pulled up out**

---

[16]   Quoted from footage of Truman speaking, presented in the film *The 50 Years War*. A slightly different quotation appears in the book, *Harry S. Truman and the Founding of Israel*, by Michael T. Benson. 1997, p. 64.

of their land, and they shall no more be pulled up out of their land which I have given them, saith the Lord thy God (Amos 9:14-15).

God's prophecy concerning the Jewish nation has become a serious subject for those who have studied the prophecies of the Bible. Now that the Jews are reestablished in their homeland, the remaining unfulfilled prophecies will happen rapidly. It is the fulfillment of this prophecy that will trigger the fulfillment of other prophecies. It is like the first domino that falls; it begins with a chain reaction that ultimately knocks over the whole row. God will begin lining up the other nations of the world in relationship to Israel.

The generation in which you and I live shall fulfill the prophecies of mankind's endeavor to dominate the earth. According to the Scriptures the world will soon witness the return of Jesus Christ. No one knows the exact day or hour but God has informed us that the reestablished Jew marks "the beginning of the end!"

CHAPTER FOUR
The Sign of the Times: Oil

The Middle East is the concern of every nation in the world. It is no surprise, considering that it is central to the economic stability of the world. World powers have, for many years, been drawn into conflicts in the Middle East. It is believed by many to be the most likely place for World War III to begin. The urgency for lasting peace and stability in that region is, therefore, of the utmost concern of every nation.

Only a few would ask the question: why is the Middle East so important? The answer is found in one word: oil. The world's economies are dependent upon Middle East oil. Oil is the stuff of life. Oil is the most valued natural resource. It is the blood that flows through the economic veins of nations and nourishes their economies. Second only to Israel, oil is the key to understanding why the Bible focuses the end times on the Middle East.

Jesus said, **"Ye can discern the face of the sky and of the earth; but how is it that ye do not discern this time?"** (Luke 12:56). Jesus contrasted the people's ability to discern the weather with their inability to discern the signs of the time. Oil, the most sought after commodity today, is buried deep in the sands of nations that are hostile to the United States. The fact that the United States is a friend to Israel qualifies as a "sign."

The world's largest crude oil reserves are located in the Middle East and North African regions. These account for 70 percent of global reserves, but only produce about 35 percent of global oil output. The members of the Organization of the Petroleum Exporting Countries (OPEC - Iran, Iraq, Kuwait, Saudi Arabia, Venezuela, Qatar, Libya, Arab Jamahiriya, United Arab Emirates, Algeria, Nigeria and Angola) hold 95 percent of the organization's existing spare oil producing capacity. In other words, they are not producing at their full capacity. The other oil producers are operating close to or at full capacity and therefore, cannot be relied upon if there is an unexpected need for greater output of oil.[17] In a global emergency, OPEC will call the shots as to oil production and cost.

OPEC is said to be entering into a new age of dominance over the oil market, the Algerian Press Service (APS) quoted the experts of the British Petroleum firm (BP) as saying. BP's forecasts show that over the next 20 years, OPEC will become as powerful as it was in the 1970s, marked by a series of oil shocks and shortages. Seventy-five percent of all growth in oil reserves over the next two decades is expected to come from OPEC nations. BP's report said that the world has become increasingly dependent on OPEC for fossil fuels, adding that the biggest growth is forecast to come from Iraq increasing its output from 2.5 million to 5.5 million barrels per day.[18]

Supply and demand of oil is not the only issue connecting the United States and the Middle East. The stability of the US dollar is connected with Arab oil. Historically, all of the world's oil has been traded in US dollars. This has guaranteed stability for the dollar and the US economy. In 1973, when oil prices drastically rose, threatening the US dollar and economy, the US entered into an agreement with Saudi Arabia, the largest oil producer, to require all oil purchases be in US dollars. In February 2008, Iran opened its own trading exchange in order to broker its own oil using Euros (the currency of the European Union). This action threatened the US dollar.

Other problems arose in oil producing countries that would affect the United States. President Hugo Chavez of Venezuela is very anti-United States. A film produced by the American Security Council Foundation focuses on the dangers America faces via Venezuela's oil-rich dictator. The film, *Crisis in the Americas,* documents the close

17   http://www.imf.org/external/pubs/ft/fandd/2003/03/okog.htm
18   http://www.malaysia-chronicle.com/index.php?option=com_k2&view=item&id=
      6672:opec-to-dominate-global-oil-market-once-again&Itemid=3

alliance Chavez shares with Iranian President Mahmoud Ahmadinejad and Chavez's eerily parallel ideologies and close coalition with Cuba's Fidel Castro. Representative Connie Mack (R-Fla.) said "My concern with Iran is Chavez wants to allow Iran to be a platform in Latin America to influence and intimidate the US, the same way that Castro did with Russia, but I think the stakes are much higher." The film trailer features security experts affirming that the US has underestimated the importance of Latin America and that Venezuela assists Iran with false identity documents that can be used for passports and Visas that will allow terrorists to enter America.[19] All of this and more can bring insecurity to the United States' oil sources and economy.

In 1973, Arab nations attacked Israel, initiating the Yom Kippur War. Yom Kippur is the holiest day in Judaism and in that year coincided with the Muslim holy month of Ramadan. The two nuclear superpowers at the time, the United States and the Soviet Union, initiated massive efforts to supply their allies. The war began on October 6 and a cease fire was agreed upon on October 25.

It was on October 17, 1973 the Arab nations would use their oil reserves as leverage against nations, primarily the United States, who favored Israel. They decreased oil production and exports. The price of a barrel of oil quadrupled. Lines formed all over the country at gas stations. The federal government passed a law minimizing the speed limit to 55 mph to conserve gas. It was a new kind of war. It was an economic war. The weapon was oil.

In August, 1990, Iraq, under the dictator, Saddam Hussein, invaded the small country of Kuwait. Their goal was to take over Kuwait's oil fields. President George H. W. Bush sent troops into Kuwait and drove back the Iraqi army. In defending his action, President Bush stated, "Our country now imports nearly half the oil it consumes and could face a major threat to its economic independence … The sovereign independence of Saudi Arabia is of vital interest to the United States."[20] It was a war over oil.

---

[19]   http://www.humanevents.com/article.php?id=22592
[20]   http://www.sweetspeeches.com/s/1429-george-h-w-bush-address-on-iraq-s-invasion-of-kuwait

Americans are once again reminded of their vulnerability over the oil issue in a recent article, entitled *Egypt and the Gas Pump: Do Revolutions Mean Higher Prices?* "Never underestimate Americans' capacity for denial. The upheaval in Egypt reminds us of lessons that, despite decades of warnings, we have consistently sidestepped: the United States and the rest of the world will depend on oil for the indefinite future, global oil markets remain hostage to political crises that cannot be predicted or controlled, and we have not taken the prudent steps that would reduce—though not eliminate—our vulnerability to catastrophic oil interruptions."[21]

Although the United States is still by far the greatest consumer of oil, more and more industrialized countries are beginning to vie for their portion of the world's supply. Using this chart as a frame of reference, the headline following the chart is very revealing:

Crude Oil Consumption by Country[22]

Rank	Country	Consumption (Thousand Barrels per Day)
1	United States	18,810.01
2	China	8,324.00
3	Japan	4,443.49
4	India	3,110.00
5	Russian Federation	2,740.00
6	Brazil	2,522.00
7	Germany	2,440.02
8	Saudi Arabia	2,438.00
9	Korea, Republic of	2,185.45
10	Canada	2,150.61
11	Mexico	2,084.15
12	France	1,827.65

21   http://www.newsweek.com/2011/02/06/egypt-and-the-gas-pump.html
22   www.indexmundi.com/energy.aspx

13	Iran, Islamic Republic of	1,691.00
14	United Kingdom	1,667.01
15	Italy	1,527.75
16	Spain	1,466.66
17	Indonesia	1,268.00
18	Netherlands	1,165.20
19	Taiwan, Province of China	971.00
20	Australia	949.78
21	Thailand	940.00
22	Singapore	927.00
23	Venezuela	723.00
24	Egypt	716.00
25	Iraq	636.00

Note the following OPEC report:

Saudi Alarmed by High Domestic Oil Demand

Official report warns local supply may not be enough in 2030

Saudi Arabia is consuming up to nearly a third of its crude oil output and supply could fail to meet domestic demand in 2030 if the high consumption trends are maintained, according to a government report.

The Gulf kingdom, the world's top oil exporter and largest Arab economy, currently produces nearly 8.5 million barrels per day of crude but local demand is as high as 2.5-3.4 million bpd, mostly used in power generation, said the report by the state-controlled Saudi Electricity Company (SEC).

The report suggested banning work of major shopping outlets during the afternoon period until 7:00 pm and limiting work periods for government departments to between 6:00 am to 12:00 noon in summer to save energy.

"The current oil production levels of around 8.5 million bpd will not be enough to meet domestic demand in 2030 if the current growth in local consumption continues," said Abdul Salam Alyamani, SEC's vice president for relations. "These high growth rates constitute a major challenge to Saudi Arabia in the long term as it relies on oil exports to provide nearly 80 per cent of its income."

How much oil do the top oil producers produce a day?[23]
- Saudi Arabia* - 8.1 million barrels per day;
  *including share of production from the Neutral Zone
- Former Soviet Union - 6.9 million barrels per day
- United States - 6.5 million barrels per day
- I.R. Iran - 3.6 million barrels per day
- China - 3.2 million barrels per day

How much oil does the world consume each day?[24]
The total world consumption of crude oil in 1996 was 71.7 million barrels per day (there are 42 US gallons in a barrel, or 159 litres). OPEC estimates that total world oil consumption could reach around 100 million barrels per day by the year 2020.

The United States' dependence on foreign oil is of great concern to all Americans. This is especially true since the oil imports we depend on are controlled by nations with which we have unstable or hostile relationships. It would be helpful and comforting if we could rely on a Middle East ally for oil—Israel.

---

[23] http://www.opec.org/faqs.html
[24] OPEC Annual Statistical Bulletin: 1996, OWEM Scenarios Report: 1998.

Former Prime Minister of Israel Golda Meir made famous the punch line to a joke told by generations of Jews. Meir said, "Let me tell you something that we Israelis have against Moses. He took us 40 years through the desert in order to bring us to the one spot in the Middle East that has no oil!" The recent findings of the Tamar and Leviathan natural gas reserves will change everything. There is an energy future for Israel.

Up until recently Israel has been unsuccessful at discovering oil reserves. It was one dry well after another, but the oil companies kept looking. There are implicit references in the Bible that many prophecy scholars believe to be of oil. The prophet Ezekiel wrote that in the end times Israel will be more prosperous than at their beginning.

> **And I will multiply upon you man and beast; and they shall increase and bring fruit: and I will settle you after your old estates, and will do better unto to you than at your beginnings: and ye shall know that I am the Lord** (Ezekiel 36:11).

Could it be possible in the last days that Israel could be more prosperous than during the reign of King Solomon?

> **They shall call the people unto the mountains; there they shall offer sacrifices of righteousness: for they shall suck of the abundance of the seas, and of treasures hid in the sand** (Deuteronomy 33:19).

Could God be referring to off-shore oil deposits when Moses prophesied and said "they shall suck of the abundance of the seas"? Was he referring to oil deposits in the ground when he said "treasures hid in the sand"? What about Moses' words:

> **Let Asher be blessed with children; let him be acceptable to his brethren, and let him dip his foot in oil** (Deuteronomy 33:24).

Consider a recent headline from Ynet News, Israel:

1.5 BILLION BARRELS OF OIL DISCOVERED NEAR ROSH HA'AYIN.

Excerpts: "Could the State of Israel be sitting on an oil reserve that can provide energy, cash flow, and international political influence? This is the question that everyone is waiting to be answered in the engineering report ordered by Givot Olam Oil, overseeing the drilling at the Megged 5 site, next to Rosh Ha'Ayin. The final report will be submitted on September 5 (2010). However, a preliminary report was already issued to Tel Aviv Stock Exchange on the oil reserves on the site. 'The amount of oil in place in Rosh Ha'Ayin plot is estimated at 1.525 billion barrels of oil.'"

Consider, too, this Ynet headline: "Israel's economy charges ahead; 4.7% growth in Q2: Israel's economic growth hits 4.7% in second quarter of 2010, leaving behind Euro bloc at 4.1%." The article notes that Israel is the fastest growing economy in the West.

All this comes on the heels of Israel's discovery of enormous reserves of natural gas. January 18, 2009: BIBLE PROPHECY UPDATE: Israel discovers "inconceivably huge quantities" of natural gas reserves off Haifa; August 19, 2009: ISRAELI NATURAL GAS DISCOVERY PROVES LARGER THAN PREVIOUSLY THOUGHT; May 15, 2010: U.S. GOVERNMENT REPORT: ISRAEL HAS 122 TRILLION CUBIC FEET OF NATURAL GAS OFFSHORE [25]

In a recent Jerusalem Post article (March, 11 2011) Dore Gold, president of the *Jerusalem Center for Public Affairs* and former Israeli

---

[25] http://flashtrafficblog.wordpress.com/2010/08/18/1-5-billion-barrels-of-oil-discovered-in-israel/

ambassador to the United Nations, stated that the fossil fuel reserves Israel discovered are the third largest oil shale deposits in the world. This could revolutionize global energy needs. Gold goes on to explain that as Middle East oil supplies from Arab countries dwindle and/or become more expensive and/or the political atmosphere becomes more contentious, Israel's exports should be available to meet needs. The bottom line, according to Gold, is Israel's exports could change the political and economic landscape in the Middle East.[26]

The discovery of oil would give Israel an immediate and considerable advantage over its Arab neighbors.

Some Christians have believed for years that prophecy suggests that oil wealth will come to Israel. They point to a desire to steal Israel's oil wealth as the trigger for the Armageddon invasion.

---

[26] http://www.oilinisrael.net/oil-in-israel-news/oil-in-israel-christian-world-news/global-energy-market

CHAPTER FIVE
Terrorism

Global terrorism and the potential use of weapons of mass destruction are a clear and present danger of immense proportions. Since time began, terrorists have had varying political and/or religious ends. In ancient times, tyrant leaders were murdered. In the Middle Ages, assassins systematically stalked and murdered their political enemies. Historically there have been those nationalists who, "for the good of the country or state," kidnap and/or murder their "oppressors." There are extremists on the left and right that ardently fight for political and/or social change.

Traditional terrorism had political and social aims. The terrorists' goal was to liberate their country from a tyrant who had taken control. They wanted independence. Perhaps they wanted to establish a new social order. At times, a terrorist's objective was forcing their antagonist into making concessions, sometimes far-reaching concessions. But today there is a new kind of terrorist. He does not have clearly defined political demands. It is a new fanaticism of religious extremism that threatens the entire world in unprecedented proportions. The terrorist of today demands the destruction of society and the elimination of large populations of people. The religious extremist's desire is the elimination of opposing believers—the infidels which may include a large part of a population, country or nationality.

Israeli Defense Minister Ehud Barak said their greatest threat is not posed by rogue states, such as Iran, even if it acquires nuclear weapons, but rather "… a nuclear weapon reaching a terrorist group, which will not hesitate to use it immediately. They will send it in a container with a GPS to a leading port in the US, Europe, or Israel."[27]

---

[27]   http://www.jewishpolicycenter.org/1745/threat-of-nuclear-terrorism

Nuclear terrorism, unlike traditional, would create a potentially catastrophic threat to nations around the world. A relatively small nuclear bomb would have devastating consequences. Thousands or tens of thousands could be killed. A total disruption of commerce and essential services, combined with shortages of food, gasoline, and medical supplies would cause widespread panic.

Nuclear terrorism poses a unique threat, not only because of the magnitude of destruction it could inflict, but more frightfully, the fact that those who would inflict such terror cannot be deterred. The new terrorist will strap a bomb to his waist and kill himself to fulfill his objectives. To these people, destroying the United States and Israel is a sacred mission. In fact, it is a part of ushering in the Islamic messiah.

What would truly be a nightmare for the world economy is a successful terrorist attack on major Saudi oil fields. An attack on Saudi Arabia, the world's largest oil producer, would cause oil to skyrocket. Such an event would be catastrophic. It would greatly impoverish developing nations, destabilize world trade and financial systems, and most likely trigger a world-wide economic recession. It may embolden terrorists to kill more civilians, topple governments and seize political power.

A documentary released in March, 2011 in Iran connects the Middle East's current unrest to the return of their messiah, Mahdi. The video openly calls for the Iranian people to wage war. The film intermixes various Islamic sacred traditions (hadith), with a hodgepodge of chanting passages from the Koran and graphic imagery portraying the Islamic world as collectively yearning for the coming of the Mahdi to deliver them from the "oppression" of the United States and Israel.

The documentary begins with the words, "Greetings to Mahdi, the one who all beings on earth and in heaven love without end. Here's the one that mirrors Allah's soul, the perfect human, the inheritor of all prophets."

The narration then moves on to the words of Imam Bahger, Shi'a Islam's fifth imam, who is quoted as saying, "The messiah [Mahdi] will not arise unless fear, great earthquakes and sedition take place."[28]

According to Islamic sacred tradition, the world will be in turmoil at the time of the Mahdi's return. There must be conflict and trouble on a global level. Turbulence and strife along with earthquakes and other signs will herald his coming, much like Christ's return. Some Muslims, like President Mahmoud Ahmadinejad of Iran, believe Muslims ought to instigate and perpetuate disorder and unrest in order to hasten the Mahdi's return. Ahmadinejad believes he has been chosen by Allah for a divine purpose, and that is to prepare the way for the Islamic 'savior' Mahdi, the 12th Imam. In almost all his speeches, Ahmadinejad begs Allah to hasten the return of the Mahdi. At a recent military parade attended by CBN News in Tehran, Ahmadinejad said, "Oh, Allah, please facilitate Imam Mahdi's early return and make us one of his supporters."

In a speech given at the United Nations Ahmadinejad said, "Oh mighty Lord, I pray to you to hasten the emergence of your last repository (a reference to the Mahdi), the promised one, that perfect and pure human being, the one that will fill this world with justice and peace." A few days later, back home in Iran, Ahmadinejad told a group of religious leaders that during his UN speech, he felt a 'bright light' around him. Ahmadinejad said, "I felt it myself. I felt that the atmosphere suddenly changed, and for those 27 or 28 minutes, all the leaders of the world did not blink. When I say they didn't move an eyelid, I'm not exaggerating. They were looking as if a hand was holding them there, and had just opened their eyes to the message of the Islamic Republic."[29]

Ahmadinejad and other Muslims, just like Christians, believe we are in the end times. Muslims believe calling for and working

---

[28]   http://www.wnd.com/index.php?fa=PAGE.printable&pageId=275909

[29]   http://www.cbn.com/cbnnews/world/2008/July/Waiting-for-Islams-Messiah-/

toward the destruction of Israel and pursuing nuclear weapons is a way to accelerate the divine timetable of their messiah, Mahdi. When the Mahdi returns it is believed by Muslims that Jesus Christ will come with him to the city of Mecca. The Mahdi will teach Jesus. Jesus will turn from the Gospel and believe the Koran. At that time all Christians will convert to Islam.

Cyber-Terrorism

There is another form of terrorism: cyber-terrorism. Cyber-terrorism is the activity of terrorists aimed at disrupting large-scale computer networks. Computer viruses are the tools of cyber-terrorists. The goal is to disrupt informational systems for the primary purpose of creating alarm and panic.

The most aggressively targeted information systems in the world are the computers and servers in the United States. Our nation's infrastructure is becoming increasingly reliant upon information technology, thus we are constantly monitoring its systems. Cyber-terrorism has the potential to affect our nation's economy, public works, transportation, communication and computer networks. Our systems are being attacked with greater frequency and sophistication by both foreign and domestic terrorists.

The threat of cyber-terrorism to the infrastructure of a nation like the United States could be devastating. Have you ever lost power in your home as a result of a storm? Has your personal computer or laptop ever "crashed?" Perhaps you lost all your information. Were you able to restore your information? If you did, it probably cost you a considerable amount of time and money, not to mention all the frustration. Magnify that a hundred trillion times and you will get some idea of the threat of cyber-terrorism to a country.

General John Gordon, former White House Homeland Security Advisor, speaking at the RSA security conference in San Francisco said, "Whether someone detonates a bomb that causes bodily harm to innocent people or hacks into a web-based IT system in a way that could, for instance, take a power grid offline and result in blackout, the result is ostensibly the same." He also stated that the potential for a terrorist cyber-attack is real.[30]

The internet makes it possible for a terrorist to affect much more damage or change to a nation than one could by blowing himself up in a supermarket. The cyber-terrorist can disable a country's military defense and destroy their economy by attacking the critical infrastructure of major cities, such as electric power grids, water supply, commendation and transportation systems.

America and the world must take Islamic terrorism seriously. We must begin, in particular with the US media, by calling it "Islamic" or "Muslim" terrorism. Although I am not a fan of his, I like what Vladimir Putin said after the Moscow bombings; speaking of the terrorists he said, "We will destroy them."

Know Your Enemies

"Know your enemy" is the first rule of war. Over the past decade Islamic terrorists have shown up in New York, London, Madrid, Bali, Mumbai, and in Moscow. They have indiscriminately killed innocent civilians on buses, trains, in subways, in skyscrapers and at resorts.

Erick Stakelbeck is an authority on terrorism and national security, and is the host of the *Stakelbeck on Terror* show on CBNNews.com. He described in his book, *The Terrorist Next Door: How the Government is Deceiving You about the Islamist,* an interview he had with Noman Benotman. Benotman, a former commander of the Islamic terrorist organization. Libyan Islamic Fighting Group, was one of the 200 jihadist leaders that met with Osama bin Laden in Afghanistan in 2000. At that meeting Osama bin Laden described his plans for a major attack against the United States that would be later known as 9/11.

---

[30] http://www.crime-research.org/articles/Cyber_Terrorism_new_kind_Terrorism/

Benotman, who left the jihadist world after 9/11, described the meeting with bin Laden in which two alQaeda leaders gleefully talked about murdering American civilians. According to the interview, Benotman warned them that such an attack on American soil would provoke a harsh response. Those present laughed and dismissed the possibility. How could they be so confident that America would take 9/11 lying down?

Benotman told Stakelbeck that jihadist leader Zawahiri and bin Laden believed the United States was a "paper tiger." They boasted about the weak responses of America to past terrorist operations. For example, the Iranian hostage crisis, the Beirut Marine barracks massacre, the 1993 World Trade Center bombing, the African embassy bombing and the USS Cole attack that killed 17 US sailors.

The US response in each attack was to issue a "strong" condemnation or simply not to respond at all. The one exception was when President Clinton, in response to the African Embassy bombing, fired a few cruise missiles into Afghanistan blowing up an empty pharmaceutical factory.

The attack on the World Trade Center would finally move American leaders to take action. The 9/11 Commission exposed the mindset that caused US political leaders for years to ignore the Islamic terrorist threat. It didn't cite past reasons for Islamic terrorism, such as poverty, mental illness, lack of education and the Israeli-Palestinian conflict and so on. According to the 9/11 Commission, it was a seductive jihadist ideology rooted in Islamic law. Erick Stakelbeck agreed, and stated in all of his interviews with current and former Islamic terrorists that it was jihadist ideology grounded in Islamic law that lubricated the terrorist machine.

During Stakelbeck's interview, Benotman stated that jihadist ideology was not a misrepresentation and distorted interpretation of Islam. As bin Laden and other terrorists maintained, Benotman said, it is grounded in the Koran itself. Benotman said, "If any Muslim appears and says ok, there is no jihad in Islam whatsoever, please believe me, he is a liar. A pure liar. People, they need to face it because it is a serious issue. Jihad, its part of Islam because it is something that's in the Koran. There are more than 40 verses, I think, in the Koran that mention jihad. Not just one or three or ten. From a Muslim perspective, the Koran is not a book written for someone or a constitution. It's the words of God."

Stakelbeck wrote, "When it comes to jihadist ideology and what motivates terrorists, who are you going to believe: a former Islamic terrorist like Noman Benotman who has rubbed shoulders with al-Qaeda's leadership, or those two-noted Islamic scholars, Eric Holder and Janet Napolitano? Call me crazy, but for a realistic assessment of the jihad threat, my money is on Benotman."[31]

---

[31] Stakelbeck, Erick, *The Terrorist Next Door: How the Government is Deceiving You About the Islamic Threat,* 2011 (Regency Publishing, 2011), pp 177-180.

CHAPTER SIX
The Invaders

"Axis of Evil" is a phrase first coined by former President George W. Bush in his January 29, 2002 State of the Union speech. Throughout his presidency, Bush often repeated it when describing the governments he accused of helping terrorists and seeking to acquire supreme power through what became known as "weapons of mass destruction." In his address to the nation the president specifically referred to Iran, Iraq and North Korea as the axis of evil. In May 2002, US Ambassador John Bolton added Libya, Syria, and Cuba to the infamous list. The president was severely criticized for his characterization of those regimes, but, interestingly, one of those nations on Bush's list is on God's list: Iran (Ezekiel 38, 39). As we proceed in this chapter we will realize that Bush's description was very appropriate.

Ezekiel 38 and 39 prophecies that soon after the restoration of the Jews in their homeland, a great enemy will rise up out of the "uttermost north" and begin an invasion of Israel.

> And from the northern part
> Comes an enemy so fierce,
> With such a hardened heart
> That pity cannot pierce.
>
> As pity cannot pierce
> He marches against God's land
> To conquer and transpierce
> The heart of every man.

The prophet Ezekiel describes this ruthless enemy as **"Gog, (of) the land of Magog, the chief prince of Meshech and Tubal ...** (Ezekiel 38:2).

TOYKO INTERNATIONAL PICTURES
PRESENTS
"GOG MEETS GODZILLA"

Over 2000 years ago
Ezekiel told of war,

How Gog from the land of Magog
And another conspirator

Would march against the Holy Land
In the "Latter Days," he said,

Bringing horror to every home,
Turning the water to blood red.

But who are Gog and Meshech?
These ancient names from the past.

Sound like a Japanese horror film—
Terrible script, cheap budget, bad cast.

Most people who read the Bible admit that they never really study it. Taking the names Gog and Magog at their face value may mean nothing to you. But I assure you, you know Gog as well as you know your own name.

In Ezekiel 38 the prophet gives us names in the family tree of this powerful invader. This allows us to trace the migrations of their descendants and discover what country they inhabit today. In Genesis we find what is commonly called the *Table of Nations* (Genesis 10). Here is a list of Noah's grandsons after the great flood through his son Japheth. Notice the names Magog, Tubal and Meshech. In those days it was a custom for descendants to name their tribes after their forefathers. Therefore the descendants of Noah's grandson Magog became known as the tribe of Magog.

The Jewish historian Josephus said that "Magog is called the Scythians by the Greeks." He continued to say that these people lived north of the Caucasus Mountains in what is known as Russia. Like Magog, the descendants of Meshech and Tubal also call themselves by their forefather's names. A fifth century B.C. Greek philosopher identified Tubal and Meshech with the Samaritans and Mushovites who lived in northern Asia Minor. The lands of both the Samaritans and the Mushovites make up parts of modern day Russia.

Wilhelm Gesenius, a famous Hebrew scholar of the nineteenth century states that Meshech was the founder of the Moschi, "a barbarous people who dwelt in the Moschian Mountains."[32] Tubal was the founder of the Tibareni, "a nation of Asia Minor, dwelling by the Euxine Sea (the Black Sea), to the west of Moschi."[33] According to Gesenius, Byzantine and Arabic writers of the same age identified Tubal and Meshech as dwelling on the river Volga. The conclusion is that these people undoubtedly are Russians.[34]

The last thing we must consider is the word "chief." This word translated is "ros," and is used not as an adjective but as a proper name as in Genesis 46: 21, "the sons of Benjamin were … Rosh." A German scholar noted that Byzantine and Arabic writers mentioned a people called Rus and Ros living in the country of Taurus among the Scythian tribes.[35] Any good history book will prove that the Scythians are a principle part of the people who make up today's Russia.

> The migration of these ancient tribes
> Is not so hard to see.
> The Bible gives the primary clue
> To trace their family tree.

---

[32] Wilhelm Gesenius, *Hebrew and Chaldee Lexicon to the Old Testament Scriptures* (Grand Rapids, MI: Wm. B. Eerdmans Publishing Company, 1974) 516.

[33] *Ibid*, p. 858 (parentheses mine)

[34] *Ibid*, p. 752

[35] www.oxfordbiblechurch.co.uk/pages/books/the-imminent-invasion-of-israel/appencix-5.php

It tells of Gog from Magog,
Meshech and Tubal too!
And Rosh, that sounds like Russian
An ironic point of view.

So take your globe, find Israel,
And not so very far
To the "uttermost north" lies and waits
The former U.S.S.R.

As the prophets had foreseen,
Gog begins a final war.
As a mighty killing machine,
He marches through their door;

He marches through their door;
Cush and Phut are by his side.
And with his conspirators,
They begin their homicide.

Allied with the "King of the North" (Gog) is the "King of the South." Daniel describes this southern commander as Egypt:

And in the end of years they shall join themselves together; ... the south shall come to the king of the north to make an agreement ... (Daniel 11:6).

Cush is the Hebrew term for the word Ethiopia (African and Arab-African countries involved with Egypt). Again we will refer to the *Table of Nations* to find the ethnic background of this southern commander.

Cush was the son of Ham. In Genesis (2:13), Moses said that "the land of Cush" was near the Tigris and Euphrates Rivers. Later, history tells us that the people from this land migrated south.

Dr. Gesenius, in his Hebrew Lexicon, says that the Cushites were black men. In Jeremiah (13:23), the Bible makes mention of the difference of their skin. Gesenius concludes by saying, "all nations sprung from Cush and enumerated in Genesis 10:7 are to be sought for in Africa."[36]

Another name we need to consider is Phut, the third son of Ham. Historians tell us his descendants migrated to the land west of Egypt and formed what we know as the North African Arab nations. Libya is the translation of the Hebrew word Phut.

Gomer was the eldest son of Japheth, and was the father of Ashenez, Riphath, and Togarmah. Ezekiel described "Gomer and his bands ..." uniting with Russia (Gog) and attacking Israel. Archaeological finds have proven that Gomer and his hordes settled north of the Black Sea and later migrated into Europe.

Dr. Gesenius describes Gomer's horde through his son Ashkenaz as "the proper name of a region and a nation in northern Asia, sprung from the Cimmerians."[37] who are the ancient people of Gomer.[38] "The modern Jews understand it to be Germany and call that country by this Hebrew name."[39] Gomer and his hordes include the area of East Germany and the Slovak countries.

> They begin their homicide
> With an ally from the east,
> Whose manpower fortified
> That numbers never cease.
>
> That numbers never cease
> Comes this destructive horde.
> The horror they release
> Will never be ignored.

---

[36]   *Ibid*, p. 389
[37]   *Ibid*, p. 86
[38]   *Ibid*, p. 856
[39]   *Ibid*, p. 86

And the sixth angel poured out his vial upon the great river Euphrates; and the water thereof was dried up, that the way of the kings of the east might be prepared (Revelation 16:12).

The original Greek words translated as "east" above are anatoles heliou, which mean, literally, "the rising of the sun." Oriental nations have always been associated with the rising sun (Japan's flag is a red sun), and the Euphrates River has always been considered to be the boundary between the east and the west.

China's power grew during the 1950s, and by the 1960s, it had gained recognition as a world power. In the February 1969 issue of *The Bulletin of Atomic Scientists*, notice was given of China's achievements in its nuclear program. The article also said that it took the Chinese less time to successfully test and fire their first H-bomb than it did the other four nuclear powers.

To spread the Communist doctrine, China began a program of military aid throughout Asia and Africa (King of the South). It was Chinese guns and equipment that the rebels used in their revolts against the governments of South Vietnam, the Congo, and Zanzibar. Today, China is arming the Middle East countries. While insisting it is not a threat to the US and her allies, China is arming Iran and other Middle East countries with advanced missile technology.

The Washington Times reported in an article, entitled *Iran's Link to China Includes Nukes, Missiles*, that recent developments confirm that China is providing Iran with defense technology and weapons systems. Iran is also receiving anti-ship missiles, nuclear technology and ballistic missile designs from Russia. This has been at the top of the United States' concerns since the fall of the Soviet Union in 1991.[40]

---

[40] http://www.washingtontimes.com/news/2010/mar/17/irans-link-to-china-in-cludes-nukes-missiles/

Another interesting clue to Gog's eastern ally is its astounding army. John, in his vision (Revelation 9:16), hears the number of men that will form this vast army—200 million. In a television documentary on Red China called "The Voice of the Dragon," the Chinese themselves boasted of how they could field an army of 200 million. So we see that the Apostle John not only prophesied that China would have a vast army, but went on to tell us that the army would consist of 200 million people. The astounding thing about this prophecy is that in John's day there weren't 200 million people in the entire world.

China has emerged after two centuries of decline as Asia's new epicenter of industry, trade, and military power. China at one time was dubbed "a slumbering giant" and the "sick man of Asia." Today, China has the world's largest army and an appetite for superiority that seems insatiable. The resurgence of China in the past century has ominous consequences for the United States and her allies. Napoleon once predicted that "when China wakes, it will shake the world." Those words are about to come true!

We are actually seeing Bible prophecy come true. Just think of it—Ezekiel, although he had no idea that there would someday be countries called Russia and China, accurately described their rise to world power.

In a dramatic challenge, China has demanded that the United States recognize it as a world power and not, as it has in the past, relegated that country to the role of a regional power. "Is the U.S. ready to recognize China as world power?" asked the headline over a major commentary in the official People's Daily newspaper. The commentary appeared in both the print and online editions, in both Chinese and English. The article quoted Secretary of State Hillary Clinton, who has urged China to play a greater role in solving the world's economic, environmental and political problems, as saying that without the participation of both China and the United States, global problems could not be solved.[41]

---

[41] http://www.koreatimes.co.kr/www/news/opinon/2011/01/171_70806.html

Americans perceive China as one of the most influential countries in the world and believe that this power and influence will grow.[42] For example, China is the largest foreign holder of US debt. On February 28, 2011 the Associated Press and CBS News reported, "China, the biggest buyer of U.S. Treasury securities, owns a lot more than previously estimated. In an annual revision of the figures, the Treasury Department said Monday that China's holdings totaled $1.16 trillion at the end of December. That was an increase of 30 percent from an estimate the government made two weeks ago."[43]

In addition, China will eventually have a military powerful enough to compete with the United States. The claim in a newspaper editorial stated that China had completed a prototype of a stealth fighter, stepped up efforts to deploy a "carrier-killer" missile system and is developing an anti-ship ballistic missiles that could pierce the defenses of even the most sturdy US naval vessels.[44]

Again we must remember that Daniel told us that the prophecies concerning the "latter days" would not be understood until the time was near for their occurrence. After all, it was only recently that the military capabilities of China were realized. And it was within this century that the Russian Empire of the mid-fifteenth century grew to be second only to the United States in world power. Some mistakenly believe that with the fall of the Soviet Union Russia ceased to be a possible threat to the United States. While the fall did diminish Russia's capabilities, it did not eliminate them. Russia still possesses a significant nuclear, chemical and biological arsenal.

Although the prophecy of Russia's invasion of the new state of Israel has yet to be fulfilled, a glance at the present alliances of Russia, Egypt, and the African countries, in relation to the Middle East conflict, is proof enough. Russia, clearly, has not lost the desire to be a world power. No one doubts that while many Russian weapon systems

---

[42] http://www.koreatimes.co.kr/www/news/opinon/2011/01/171_70806.html
[43] http://www.cbsnews.com/8301-503983_162-20037535-503983.html
[44] http://www.channelnewsasia.com/stories/afp_asiapacific/view/1103305/1/.html

are still aimed at the United States and Iran has promised to destroy Israel, this country obviously still presents a threat to Israel.

CHAPTER SEVEN
The Antichrist

"The devil hath the power to assume a pleasing shape."
William Shakespeare, Hamlet

I saw Christ in Kansas City,
And again in Omaha.

He was interviewed in Boston
And he preached in Montreal.

I saw his picture in the *Post*
And in *People* magazine.

I thought he came from Taiwan,
But the *Post* said Argentine.

I heard his hair was wavy,
But the *Tribune* shows it flat.

The *New York Times* says he's bald
On NBC he wore a hat.

Some heard he was a black man;
Others say he's red.

Some believe his name is Manson;
In New Orleans he's known as Fred.

Throughout Christ's ministry, especially as the time of the cross neared, He warned his disciples of false prophets, teachers and messiahs. In Matthew 24 Jesus tells His disciples what the major signs of His coming and the end of the world will be. In that chapter there are several references that warn us of those who will appear in the final days claiming to be prophets sent from God, and even claiming to be Jesus Himself. Common sense tells us that since Jesus made such a point to remind us of these "pretenders" it must have been for good reason. Today we can clearly understand why. With the mass communication of today it is not inconceivable to believe that a false prophet could preach his deceptive message to the world. Never before have these impersonators had such a perfect generation in which to thrive.

Some of the prophecies that described events, situations and technologies hundreds or even thousands of years in the future made little sense to the prophets themselves. Most of their predictions could only be understood by a person living in a modern technologically advanced world—our world of air travel, satellites, mass communication, bombs, missiles, computers and so on.

Thousands of years ago, God's prophets foretold of a time when the ability to communicate would be instant and on a world-wide scale. They foretold of a world where communication and public opinion could be manipulated by religious, economic and political means. This remarkable capacity to communicate and manipulate a message would culminate in the rise of a world dictator—the Antichrist. The Bible gives a variety of names to the man called Antichrist. The term Antichrist simply means against Christ. To the world the Antichrist will be a savior. He will be a pseudo-Christ. He will be Satan's counterfeit Christ, a false Messiah. The world will fall in love with this man. It will be a deception so powerful that true believers will be silenced, persecuted and murdered. Christians, like Jews during World War II, will be murdered while the complacent attitude of the public will be that it is best for society.

Do you find this hard to believe? The prophecies of the two witnesses of Revelation 11 lay the groundwork for this shocking scenario:

And I will give power unto my two witnesses and they shall prophecy a thousand two hundred and threescore days ... (v. 3) **And when they shall have finished their testimony, the beast (antichrist) ... shall overcome them, and kill them** (v.7). **And their dead bodies shall lie in the street of the great city ...** (v. 8). **And they of the people and kindreds and tongues and nations shall see their dead bodies ...** (v. 9). **And they that dwell upon the earth shall rejoice over them, and make merry, and shall send gifts one to another; because these two prophets tormented them that dwell on the earth** (v. 10).

Daniel, who lived 600 years before Jesus Christ, foretold of a time when people would travel over great distances and speeds. He saw into the future an information explosion. Although Daniel did not understand the meaning of his predictions, God revealed to him that believers near the end will understand; **"none of the wicked shall understand; but the wise shall understand"** (Daniel 12:10).

The angel said, "But thou, O Daniel, shut up the words, and seal the book, even to the time of the end: many shall run to and fro, and knowledge shall be increased" (Daniel 12:4).

God told Daniel to "Shut up the words, and seal the book"; close the book **"even to the time of the end."** Why should the book be closed until the time of the end? Because the predictions describe a technological world that even 100 years ago would have been inconceivable. Man's technology must catch up before he will understand. "Many shall run to and fro" is an obvious reference to the rapid mass transportation that will be common in the last days. **"And knowledge shall be increased"** refers to the expansion of science and technology in the last days.

The primary medium of knowledge occurred in the 18th century "age of enlightenment" with the invention of the printing press. In the 19th century, public education brought widespread literacy which furthered technological progress. In the 20th century, technological advancements in electronic communication exploded bringing radio, television, computers, satellites and ultimately the internet. The internet makes possible all the advancements in technology available to anyone in their home 24 hours a day and 7 days a week. Information and images can now be disseminated literally in seconds to any place on earth.

Without these great advances in technology, the prophecy of the two witnesses would be impossible to understand. There are two things about these witnesses that can only be understood in our modern day. First, the world hears their message and second, sees their murder and resurrection.

> **And I will give power unto my two witnesses, and they shall prophesy (preach) a thousand two hundred and threescore days, clothed in sackcloth. These have power to shut heaven, that it rain not in the days of their prophecy: and have power over waters to turn them to blood, and to smite the earth with all plagues, as often as they will.**

> **And when they shall have finished their testimony, the <u>beast</u> that ascendeth out of the bottomless pit shall make war against them, and shall overcome them, and kill them. And their dead bodies shall lie in the street of the great city, which spiritually is called Sodom and Egypt, where also our Lord was crucified. And <u>they</u> of the people and kindreds and tongues and nations shall <u>see</u> their dead bodies three days and an half, and shall not suffer their dead bodies to be put in graves.**

And they that dwell upon the earth shall rejoice over them, and make merry, and shall send gifts one to another; because these two prophets tormented them that dwelt on the earth.

And after three days and an half the Spirit of life from God entered into them, and they stood upon their feet; and great fear fell upon them which <u>saw</u> them. And they heard a great voice from heaven saying unto them, Come up hither. And they ascended up to heaven in a cloud; and their enemies beheld them (Revelation 11:3-12, underline mine).

John predicts a worldwide conflict in which the beast, the Antichrist, will rise to power by manipulating public opinion and religious deception using the media. Although the people of the world will not believe the message of the two witnesses, they will hear and see them via radio, television and the internet. Pictures of the two witnesses being killed and their bodies lying in the street will be broadcast around the world. People of the nations will be happy that they are dead; the message they preached "tormented them" (v.12).

Daniel foretells of four mighty empires, the first and second coming of Jesus Christ and the charismatic dictator who will oppose God's people and the Lord Jesus Christ (Daniel 2, 7, 8-9, 11-12). This man will emerge out of a world of economic, political and religious chaos and discontentment. People all over the world will long for peace and economic security. And when someone arrives on the scene and offers an answer to all these problems he will be the one to gain attention from the crowds.

"The streets of our country are in turmoil; the universities are filled with students rebelling and rioting; Communists are seeking to destroy our country, and the Republic is in danger—yes, danger from within and without! We need law and order! Without law and order our nation cannot survive."[45]

---

[45]   Http://www.babson.us/quotes/html

Those words were spoken in 1932 by Adolph Hitler. Are you surprised? The remarkable thing about them is that leaders in the United States, Europe, Africa, South America, and Asia could now say similar things concerning the social, economical and political conditions of their own countries.

A dictator rarely walks into another nation's capitol and announces that he will take over without provocation. The ground from which dictatorial power grows must be fertilized with anarchy, lawlessness, social and economic depression, and human desperation. These are the conditions upon which the seed of a dictator thrives. Therefore, it can be understood that it is the troubled society, and not the man per se, that produces the atmosphere ripe for a dictator.

The German people were in despair in the 1930s. Germany was economically unstable and her industries were crumbling. Crime was rampant. The German people felt a hopelessness that laid the groundwork for a dictatorial takeover. These were the same conditions prevalent right before smaller countries were taken over by Caesar and his Great Roman Empire. The people of those countries were actually grateful to Caesar because Roman law was soon established and chaos was eliminated. This ultimately led them to worship Caesar.

Adolph Hitler, knowing the mood of the German people, arrived on the scene at just the right time. His personality and oratorical abilities mesmerized thousands. His speeches promised an economic rebirth for Germany and, in a time of frustration and joblessness, the people made him their leader.

World Conditions

> Economic emergency!
> Chaos is on the way.
> Social disorder is on the rise;
> Depression is here to stay.

The crime rate has arisen;
This is a hopeless trend.
You may be robbed at the bus stop
Or murdered by your best friend.

World population is a threat;
There's starving by the multitudes.
And the crime rate rises higher
As we rob our neighbor's food.

Chemicals threaten our rivers;
Their banks are lined with debris.
And the very oil we're trying to save
Is polluting our rivers and sea

Racial tensions increasing;
Minorities under attack.
If you're not born of the dominant group,
You're going to be held back.

Trying to solve our problems,
Scientists worldwide are involved.
But the ironic fact about science
Is it's created more problems than solved.

They've produced a vaccine for polio
And sprays that come in a can,
Nuclear energy for heating our homes,
Could cause the extinction of man.

We know more about economics,
But there's more poverty than ever before.
Starvation is rampant and climbing,
Poor people just keep getting poorer.

Youth suicide is frightful
In this world of uncertainty and strife.
Abortion and an increase of murders
Prove our failing reverence for life.

We're treading a sea of troubles
With a collar made of lead,
And the threat of drowning is like the sword
Of Damocles over our head.

Countries around the world are experiencing the same economic, social, and political depressions that the German people experienced before the rise of Adolph Hitler. It is evident that nearly all countries that have ultimately been seduced by a dictator have experienced these truths.

European nations are facing financial bankruptcy and social unrest. One European statesman was quoted as saying "if the devil could offer a panacea for the problems of the world, I would gladly follow the devil."[46] At this point there is no way of knowing whether this man was serious or joking, but it is ironic that the Bible predicts that this is exactly what will happen. In the near future, when the world can no longer solve its own problems, a charismatic individual will step onto the world's stage. He will be welcomed and loved by the nations. He will be the greatest of all political leaders. He will be considered to be god-like and will seem to have all the answers to the problems that plague modern day man.

And he shall speak great words against the most High, and shall wear out the saints of the most High, and think to change times and laws: and they shall be given into his hand ... (Daniel 7:25).

---

[46]   http://www.ccel.us/worldaflame.ch1.html

The Beast Out of the Sea

This vivid description from Revelation 13:1-4 could be the opening scene of a modern day horror film, and yet it is the revelation of conditions on the earth at the end of this age:

> **And I stood upon the sand of the sea, and saw a beast rise up out of the sea, having seven heads and ten horns, and upon his horns ten crowns, and upon his heads the name of blasphemy. And the beast which I saw was like unto a leopard, and his feet were as the feet of a bear, and his mouth as the mouth of a lion: and the dragon gave him his power, and his seat, and great authority. And I saw one of his heads as it were wounded to death; and his deadly wound was healed: and all the world wondered after the beast. And they worshipped the dragon which gave power unto the beast; and they worshipped the beast, saying, "Who is like unto the beast? Who is able to make war with him?"** (Revelation 13:1-4).

Revelation 13 is perhaps one of the most famous and well known chapters in all of Bible prophecy. Many people, Christians and non-Christians alike, are familiar with it. Its popularity is due to its symbolism and colorful descriptions of something concerning the future, and mankind is always curious about the future.

The Antichrist or, as some have called him, "the Future Fuehrer," is referred to as a "beast." The beast is said to rise up out of the sea or the nations. This interpretation is made clear by John in Revelation 17:15. The sea represents the chaos of people and nations in the final days. **"The waters which thou sawest … are peoples, and multitudes, and nations, and tongues"** (Revelation 17:15). The prophet Isaiah said of the beast rising out of the sea **"The wicked are like the troubled sea"** (Isaiah 57:20). Three things identify the beast as a human being: verse 5, "speaking," verse 7, "power was given him to rule over all" (animals neither talk nor rule countries), and, finally, use of the personal pronoun "he" throughout the chapter, obviously referring to a person.

The dictionary describes "beast" as having "qualities or impulses like an animal's; a person who is brutal, gross, vile." Daniel tells us he will persecute Christians, **"... and shall wear out the saints of the most High"** (Daniel 7:25). Because of the horror and brutality that this man will cause, God Himself refers to him as a "beast."

> The sea is never peaceful;
> Unruly, full of strife,
> Nervous, always moody,
> Depicts a churning strife.
>
> And so are we as people
> So like the troubled sea,
> Never calm and tranquil,
> Just constant calamity.

And the beast which I saw was like unto a leopard, and his feet were as the feet of a bear, and his mouth as the mouth of a lion (Revelation 13:2).

And four great beasts came up from the sea, diverse one from another. These great beasts, which are four, are four kings, which shall arise out of the earth (Daniel 7:3, 17).

The prophet Daniel tells us of four beasts rising out of the chaos of nations. Each one is different from the other. He continues in verse 17 by telling us that the beasts represent four kings or world leaders who will come to power sometime in the future.

The first was like a lion ... And behold another beast, a second like a bear ... (Daniel 7:4-5).

Babylon: The Lion

Babylon is where the prophet Daniel lived, and he described it as the first of the four kingdoms that would rule over the entire earth. Babylon became a world power in 606 B.C. It is described as a lion. The lion, which is called the "king of beasts," is a proud and arrogant animal; the Babylonian Empire was considered a proud and arrogant monarchy. Famous for its luxury and wealth, the city of Babylon was once considered one of the *Seven Wonders of the World.*

Medes & Persians: The Bear

About 530 B.C. the Medes and the Persians conquered the Babylonian Empire becoming the second great kingdom to come to power. It was considered a strong and powerful empire, which is why it has been compared to the bear.

In Daniel 8 we read about a fierce battle between a ram and goat. The goat easily defeats the ram. In verses 20 and 21 Daniel interprets the symbolism of the ram and the goat, **"The ram which thou sawest having two horns are the kings of Media and Persia. And the rough goat is the king of Grecia."**

Greece: The Leopard

> **After this I beheld, and lo another, like a leopard, which had upon the back of it four wings of a fowl; the beast had also four heads; and dominion was given to it** (Daniel 7:6).

Once again we see an example of the accuracy of a true prophet of God. Greece became the third country to rule the entire earth after conquering the Median and Persian Empire. Notice that in Daniel 8:5 the goat, who was the king of Greece, has a **"notable horn between his eyes."** In verse 21 the interpretation of that horn is **"the first king."** Then in verse 22: **"Now that being broken** (meaning that the horn

THE SECOND COMING OF JESUS CHRIST

is broken, or the first king dies), **whereas four stood up for it, four kingdoms will stand up out of the nation, but not in his power."** After the death of the first king, four leaders will rise up out of the Greek Empire, dividing the empire among them. But it will not be as powerful a nation as it originally was under the first king. Alexander the Great, perhaps one of the most ambitious young kings who ever lived. This amazing prophecy was fulfilled nearly 200 years later.

We see that this third kingdom is said to be like a leopard. Alexander the Great stormed across the Granicus River with his cavalry and conquered the Persians. This was why Daniel compared the Greek Empire to the Leopard—because it, too, was quick to seize its prey.

Summing it Up

In Daniel 8:20, 21 we have definite proof of the first three world powers. Any student of history will be familiar with the conquest of Persia by the Greeks. Therefore all we need to do is to find out who the Medes and Persians conquered to become the rulers of the world to identify the first beast that was "like a lion." History says Babylon.

> Of all the beasts that Daniel predicted,
> None has been so horribly depicted
> As beast number four who conquered the Greek.
> Unlike the others, its character unique,
> It walked like a lion, arrogant and proud
> Swift like a leopard, like the bear was its growl,
> Possessed with power till its mouth ran with foam,
> Not Babylon, or Persia, nor Greece, but Rome.

Behold a fourth beast, dreadful and terrible, and strong exceedingly ... (Daniel 7:7).

Rome: Compared to No Animal

This is the fourth beast, so terrible that the Bible does not relate it to a specific animal. It is more powerful than the first three world conquerors. Rome conquered the Greek empire to become the most powerful empire in the entire known world. The Great Roman Empire reigned longer than any nation to date before its tragic fall.

What does Daniel's prophecy of these now ancient civilizations have to do with the beast (Antichrist) of the future in Revelation 13? Notice what that chapter says in verse 2: **"And the beast which I saw was like unto a leopard … a bear … a lion"** The Apostle John uses the same animals to describe the beast of the future as the prophet Daniel uses to describe the beasts, or world conquerors, of our past. The reason is that the characteristics of the future beast (the Antichrist) are the same. The Antichrist will be arrogant and wondered after like Babylon, powerful and destructive like the Medes and Persians, and quick to seize its prey like the Greek Empire.

> The beast is hidden behind the door
> Cracked ever so slightly, his eyes explore.
>
> Lurking nervously among the crowd,
> Waiting to pounce from behind a shroud.
>
> He may be a neighbor or may be a friend.
> We're certain he's living—it's nearing the end.
>
> He'll probably smile when he reads this poem.
> The Bible predicts he'll ascend out of Rome.

The fourth beast (the Roman Empire) of Daniel's prophecy is not mentioned in verse 2 of Revelation 13, as are the first three world conquerors. Referring to chapter 7 in Daniel, in the "last days," there will be a second phase of the Roman Empire. The fact that the Roman Empire will reemerge in the last days is one of the ways in which the fourth beast is "diverse" from the first three (verse 7). As we continue to read we see that Daniel's fourth beast has ten horns—the same number as the beast in Revelation 13, verse 1. This is evidence that the fourth beast in Daniel is the same as the one prophesied by the Apostle John in Revelation. Verse 24 confirms this: **"And the ten horns out of this kingdom are ten kings that shall arise."**

The words "out of" mean the ten nations or ten kings will come out of the cultural inheritance of the Great Roman Empire. They are not referring to a physical or geographical revival of the Roman Empire, but to the culture, nations, and people that were a part of the original empire.

After these ten nations rise out of the cultural inheritance of Rome **"another shall arise after them: and he shall be diverse from the first"** Daniel 7:24). This is undoubtedly the Antichrist, who will rise up out of these ten nations. He will be different from the other ten rulers (presidents, etc) because he will be given full control.

> **And he shall subdue three kings. And he shall speak great words against the most High ... and think to change times and laws: and they shall be given unto his hand** (Daniel 8:24, 25).

From these verses we learn that the Antichrist will rise up out of these ten nations. Seven of these countries will follow him willingly while the other three must be taken by force. He will be different in that he will not only be a political leader but a spiritual leader as well. The entire world scene will be affected by this man. If we turn back to Revelation we'll learn how the Antichrist will come to such heights of power.

> **And the dragon gave him his power, and his seat, and great authority"** (Revelation 13:2).

> Who is this dragon
> That gives him power
> To grow from a child

And eventually devour
The entire political scene?

What is this monster
That breathes out fire
And grants this man
What 'ere he desire
In the world and on the sea?

Why is it given unto a man
Authority to rule an entire Land?
Where is this dragon?
What's in his hand?
What is this dragon today?

And the great dragon was cast out, that old serpent, called the devil, and Satan (Revelation 12:9).

And I saw one of his heads as if it was wounded to death; and his deadly wound was healed: and all the world wondered after the beast. And they worshiped the dragon which gave power unto the beast: and they worshiped the beast ... and power was given him over all kindreds, and tongues, and nations (Revelation 13:3, 7).

If someone asked you what you considered to be the greatest miracle that anyone could perform, what would you say? Almost everyone would agree that making a person that has died rise up and live again would be the greatest feat ever performed. Hypothetically, consider this: the day after Winston Churchill's death he suddenly rose up out of his coffin declaring he was God! As prominent a person as he was, can you imagine the worldwide following he would attract after having risen from the dead? No doubt he would be worshiped as the living God. This is exactly how the Antichrist will come into power. But read carefully the words *as if*, meaning that the Antichrist will be wounded and appear to be dead. It will be part of a great deception.

He will not really be dead, but the power given to him from Satan will make him appear to have died and returned to life.

And so we find that Satan himself gives this man these remarkable powers to seduce the world. This man, who is the Antichrist, literally sells his soul to the devil in exchange for world leadership. If you recall, Jesus, after being in the desert for many days, was approached by Satan with the same offer.

And the devil, taking him up into an high mountain, showed unto him all the kingdoms of the world ... And the devil said unto him, All this power will I give thee, and the glory of them: ... If thou therefore wilt worship me, all shall be thine (Luke 4:5-7).

Whereas Christ rebuked Satan, the Antichrist will not.

The European Common Market: Ten Nations Strong

According to Daniels' prophecy, a ten-nation confederacy will rise to power out of the culture of the Great Roman Empire. This prophecy is now a fact. The European Common Market is a world superpower. The European Common Market is definitely not only an economic power but a political power that must be reckoned with by today's world.

The European Union: The Future Base of Antichrist

The European Union (UE) is made up of over 25 countries. Ten of those nations have a separate status as full members. The other nations have only an associate membership status. This is the fulfillment of the prophecy of the ten beasts with ten horns (Daniel 7:7-8 and Revelation 13:1).

On this beast's back rides a woman. This woman is a symbol of a worldwide religious system that is to appear before Christ returns.

So he carried me away in the spirit into the wilderness: and I saw a woman sit upon a scarlet coloured beast, full of names of blasphemy, having seven heads and ten horns (Revelation 17:3).

The symbol of a woman riding on the back of a beast is shown on the stamp of the European Union.

Stamp

The European Union's chosen symbol is a woman riding on a beast.

Sculpture outside the Council of Ministers Office in Brussels, Belgium

Cover of May 2000 Der Spiegel magazine

Time magazine's United Europe

European coinage, the Euro, bears the same insignia of a woman riding a beast.

2002 2 Euro coin

1996 5 Euro coin

Photo below of Condoleezza Rice at the United Nations in 2005 with the numbers 666 behind her. Notice how the logo below was cleverly designed, celebrating the UN's 60th anniversary.

Empty Seat Number 666[48]

The *Tower Building* (named after the *Tower of Babel*) houses the Fifth Parliament of Europe. It is certainly a building of the Space Age. The seats are designed like the crew seats in Star *Trek* space machines. The legislative amphitheater is arranged in a massive circle and has 679 seats, each assigned to a particular lawmaker. For example, Seat 663 is assigned to Rep Souchet, 664 to Thomas-Mauro, 665 to Zizzner and 667 to Rep Cappato.

While these seats are allocated to Members, **one seat remains unallocated and unoccupied**. The number of that seat is 666. The relevant section of the seating-plan provided to each Member reads as follows:

660 Marchiani
661 Montfort
662 Quiero
663 Souchet
664 Thomas-Mauro
665 Zizzner
666 -------
667 Cappato
668 Turco
669 Bonino
670 Pannella

47   http://un.org/un60/media_oct24.html
48   http://www.jesus-is-savior.com/endoftheworld/seat/666.html

671 Dupuis
672 Della Vedova

Revelation 13:18 states: **"Here is wisdom. Let him that hath understanding count the number of the beast: for it is the number of a man; and his number [is] six hundred threescore [and] six."**

CHAPTER EIGHT
The Rapture

When I was growing up at First Baptist Church in Fairview Heights, Illinois, there was a beloved woman named Violet Hanks. Violet played the piano on Sunday morning and evening. She played magnificently. No one could play the piano like Violet. She not only played but also wrote beautiful music and lyrics. My favorite Violet Hanks song was one that my wife Pamela sang; accompanied by Violet on the piano. The title of the song was *In The Twinkling Of An Eye* and it was inspired by the Apostle Paul's words in First Corinthians, chapter fifteen.

Behold, I show you a mystery; We shall not all sleep, but we shall all be changed, In a moment, *in the twinkling of an eye*, at the last trump: for the trumpet shall sound, and the dead shall be raised incorruptible, and we shall be changed (1 Corinthians 15:51-52, italics mine).

In The Twinkling Of An Eye
By Violet Hanks

In the twinkling of an eye
I'll see my Jesus.
In the twinkling of an eye
I'll see my Lord.
Oh, yes the trumpet will be heard
With voice supernal.
Oh, He calleth for His own,
Bids them enter a new home
In the twinkling of an eye.

In the twinkling of an eye
When I'm with Jesus.
In the twinkling of an eye
When I'm with my Lord.
He will wipe away the tears
Of earthly sorrow,
And with loved ones I will be
Oh, what joy waits for me
In the twinkling of an eye.

In the twinkling of an eye
I'll be like Jesus.
In the twinkling of an eye
I'll be like Him.
This old body will be changed
For life eternal
Like my Savior I will be
Clothed in immortality
In the twinkling of an eye.

This will happen
In a twinkling of an eye.

On April 19, 2011 in McKeesport, Pennsylvania, structural concerns forced the evacuation of a McKeesport apartment building. WTAE Channel 4 Action News reported that 13 people, including six children, had to leave the building in the 400 block of Shaw Avenue. The owner told WTAE he noticed bricks were coming apart and contacted the fire department, prompting the evacuation. One resident said, "I'm happy they got us out before the building collapsed."[49]

What if you lived in that apartment building and you somehow didn't get the message to evacuate? Can you image awakening in the middle of the night as the apartment building you live in starts crumbling around you? As you make your way through the blinding, choking dust

---

[49]   http://www.wtae.com/news/27605150/detail.html

and falling plaster you finally make it outside to safety. Standing in the yard you notice you are the only resident of the building that was still inside. You learn the fire department had previously evacuated all of the residents earlier except for you. You are amazed and wonder why you were left behind.

In the last days before the return of Jesus Christ, there is going to be a worldwide evacuation of Christians. It is called the Rapture. The Rapture, a word that means to be suddenly caught up, refers to an event described in 1 Thessalonians 4:17 when believers will be gathered together in the air to meet Jesus Christ.

> **Then we which are alive and remain shall be caught up together with them in the clouds, to meet the Lord in the air: and so shall we ever be with the Lord** (1 Thessalonians 4:17).

The purpose of that evacuation is the same as when they evacuated the residents of the apartment building in McKeesport. The residents were to vacate the building in order to avoid a catastrophe. Jesus Christ will rapture Christians from all over the world in order that they will avoid the upcoming period known as the Tribulation. The focus of the Rapture is not on those that remain but on those who are caught up—evacuated.

> **Let not your heart be troubled: ye believe in God, believe also in me. In my Father's house are many mansions: if it were not so, I would have told you. I go to prepare a place for you. And if I go and prepare a place for you, I will come again, and receive you unto myself; that where I am, there ye may be also** (John 14:1-3).

There are two major events that will occur with regard to the Second Coming of Jesus Christ, and they are commonly misunderstood and confused. The first event is called the Rapture, and this will happen secretly and covertly. Unbelievers who are left behind will be unaware of the Rapture. Confusion and panic will ensue all over the world. Reports of missing relatives and friends will flood police stations. People will not know what happened to friends, loved ones and co-workers who just vanished without a trace. Believers will be transported by Jesus to heaven.

> **Then shall two be in the field; the one shall be taken, and the other left. Two women shall be grinding at the mill; the one shall be taken, and the other left** (Matthew 24:40, 41).

The Second Coming will occur seven years later when Jesus literally returns to the earth accompanied by the believers who were caught up in the Rapture. The Second Coming will happen openly and publically.

> **Behold, he cometh with clouds; and every eye shall see him, and they also which pierced him: and all kindreds of the earth shall wail because of him. Even so, Amen** (Revelation 1:7, see also Zechariah 14:1, 3-5; Revelation 19:11-21).

There will be many signs of Christ's Second Coming (Matthew 24). There will be no signs leading up to the Rapture. The Rapture will happen suddenly and without warning. The Rapture and The Second Coming can be compared to Thanksgiving and Christmas. We see many signs of Christmas approaching, often very early, as malls and shopping centers stock their shelves and decorate for Christmas. Weeks in advance of Christmas people decorate their lawns and houses with lights, figures and Christmas trees. People do not decorate for Thanksgiving. Before you know it, Thanksgiving has arrived and then you know for certain that Christmas is very near. But even with great advance warning, many people are simply not prepared when Christmas Eve arrives.

In a similar way, when you begin seeing the signs of Jesus' Second Coming you know the time is near, even at the door (Matthew 24:33). And when you see those signs of the Second Coming you can know the Rapture is even nearer because it comes seven years before the Second Coming.

In the first three chapters of Revelation we find many references to the church on earth. From chapter 4 through chapter 18 there is no mention of the church. In fact, it is conspicuous by its absence. The fact that the church is not present during the horrors of the Tribulation is a pattern which God has followed throughout history. For instance, when God decided to destroy the earth by water He warned Noah and told him how to prepare for the flood (Genesis 6:7-14). Before God destroyed the ancient cities of Sodom and Gomorrah, He warned Lot to flee from the cities (Genesis 19:12-13). Before God sent the death angel to Egypt, He warned the Israelites and instructed them how to protect themselves (Exodus 4-6, 12-13). In these instances God warned His people of the oncoming judgments so they would not have to suffer with the ungodly. The pattern was always the same—God's warning, evacuation of His people, then destruction.

The Apostle Paul gives us an important clue concerning the rapture of God's people:

> **Flesh and blood cannot inherit the kingdom of God … Behold, I show you a mystery; We shall not all sleep, but we shall all be changed, in a moment, in the twinkling of an eye, at the last trump: for the trumpet shall sound, and the dead shall be raised incorruptible, and we shall be changed** (1 Corinthians 15:50-52).

Jesus makes a profound statement in Matthew's Gospel:

> **Verily I say unto you, there be some standing here, which shall not taste of death, till they see the Son of Man coming in his kingdom** (Matthew 26:28).

The word "sleep" is used throughout the Scriptures to mean Christian death. Many people believe that the word sleep means that your soul goes to a place called "limbo" where you wait until the last days when Christ returns to raise your body from the grave. On the contrary, the Bible teaches that the moment you breathe your last breath you are instantly transported into the presence of God (2 Corinthians 5:8).

The Second Coming is Jesus' literal and physical return to the earth at the end of the Great Tribulation. The term "Great Tribulation" refers to the second half of the Tribulation period. During the first 3½ years the Antichrist will bring a pseudo-peace to the world. The second 3½ years, beginning with the Antichrist's desecration of the Jewish temple (see Chapter 3, *The Key to the Prophetic Puzzle*), will be a time of great war and the Battle of Armageddon. It will close with the Second Coming of Jesus Christ. Jesus will usher in a time known as the Millennium—a thousand year reign of Jesus Christ upon the earth. The Rapture will occur seven years prior to Jesus' Second Coming.

The Second Coming will also occur at the height of a global battle called Armageddon. If it were not for Jesus' Second Coming the people of the world would destroy themselves.

And except those days should be shortened, there should no flesh be saved ... (Matthew 24:22).

Compare the Rapture and the Second Coming

The Rapture	The Second Coming
When will it occur?	
Before the Tribulation (Revelation 3:10).	After the Tribulation (Matthew 24:29-30).

How will it occur?	
In a moment in the twinkling of an eye (1 Corinthians 15:52). People will not know what happened.	Gradual. People everywhere know what is happening (Matthew 24:27; Revelation 1:7).
What are the signs?	
There are no signs.	There are many signs (Matthew 24:1-28).
Will it be visible?	
Believers will see Christ (1 John 3:2).	Every person will see Christ (Revelation 1:7).
Where will Christ come?	
Christ will not come to earth. He will meet believers in the air (1 Thessalonians 4:17).	His feet touch down on the Mt. of Olives (Zechariah 14:4; see also Acts 1:11).
Who will be taken?	
Believers will be taken; unbelievers will be left. (1 Thessalonians 4:13-18).	Believers will be left. Unbelievers will be taken away in judgment (Luke 17:34-37).
Why Does He Come?	
To receive His bride which is the Church (John 14:3).	To receive His kingdom (Luke 19:12).

The rapture and second coming are similar but separate events. Both involve Jesus returning. Both are end-times events. The rapture is the return of Christ in the clouds to remove all believers from the earth before the time of God's wrath. The second coming is the return of Christ to the earth to defeat the Antichrist and bring the Tribulation to an end.

> **For then shall be great tribulation, such as was not since the beginning of the world to this time, no, nor ever shall be** (Matthew 24: 21-22).

The word tribulation is defined as "great misery or distress … deep sorrow." The Tribulation, as this period is called, will be a time of suffering and sorrow like the world has never known. Had Jesus not promised to return, mankind would not survive.

CHAPTER NINE
The Seven Seals

Revelation 6 describes the events taking place in heaven following the Rapture. This begins with the opening of seven seals, and as each seal is opened, judgments are released upon the earth. The Seven Seals is a phrase used to refer to the symbolic seals that seal the "book" or "scroll" that John saw in his Revelation of Jesus Christ. As each seal is opened, judgment is released on the earth.

The First Seal

The first seal is opened; the Tribulation officially begins. The Antichrist begins his conquest.

> **And I saw when the Lamb opened one of the seals, and I heard, as it were the noise of thunder, one of the four beasts saying, "Come and see." And I saw, and behold a white horse: and he that sat on him had a bow; and a crown was given unto him: and he went forth conquering, and to conquer** (Revelation 6:1, 2).

The first significant event of the future Tribulation will be the emergence of Antichrist, symbolized here as the rider on a white horse. In this instance, this is a human being who, energized by Satan, begins his campaign of world conquest. He does not appear as a horrible or evil monster, but as a benevolent dictator. He is seen as a messiah, who has come to solve the world's great problems.

Earlier we described a man who will be so ruthless that he will make Hitler's persecution of Jews seem trivial. He will literally sell his soul to the devil in exchange for world power. This man on the white horse is the Antichrist himself. The white horse symbolizes conquest by its rider. At the end of the Tribulation when we find another rider on a white horse, it will be Jesus Christ who comes to conquer at His Second Coming (Revelation 19:11-21).

Throughout history kings and generals have always gone into battle riding a white steed. This messianic-like person carries a bow, symbolizing his great authority and control over mankind and the weapons of the world. Notice the phrase, **"a crown was given to him."** The Antichrist, like all dictators, will be given his authority by the people themselves. They will recognize him as a great world leader. This man will have proven himself to be a great leader of men. He will have brought peace to the uncompromising Middle East crisis and successfully explained the absence of millions of Christians who have mysteriously vanished. By this time he will have won the hearts of billions. In Daniel 9:27 we find the beginning of the tribulation, with the Antichrist signing a peace agreement with Israel. It is at this point that the Jews reestablish the temple that was destroyed by the Romans 2000 years ago, and resume offering sacrifices unto God.

The Second Seal

> **And when he had opened the second seal, I heard the second beast say, Come and see. And there went out another horse that was red: and power was given to him that sat thereon to take peace from the earth, and that they should kill one another: and there was given unto him a great sword** (Revelation 6:3, 4).

During the first three and one-half years of the tribulation there will be a pseudo-peace throughout the world. The Antichrist will have gained world recognition for his achievement of world peace. No doubt, he will be the recipient of the Nobel Peace Prize. As predicted, the balance of power will suddenly shift as God proves that the promises of the Antichrist cannot stand.

At this point two major events will take place. The Antichrist **"shall cause the sacrifice and the oblation to cease"** (Daniel 9:27).

This means that the Antichrist will enter the newly rebuilt temple in Jerusalem and proclaim himself God. This was prophesied by Daniel, Jesus, and the Apostle Paul.

> **Who opposeth and exalteth himself above all that is called God, or that is worshiped; so that he as God sitteth in the temple of God, showing himself that he is God** (2 Thessalonians 2:4).

The king of the south (Arab-African confederacy headed by Egypt) will now invade Israel accompanied by his ally, the King of the North (Russia/Gog). The Armageddon campaign will have officially begun.

> [9] **Thou shalt ascend and come like a storm, thou shalt be like a cloud to cover the land, thou, and all thy bands, and many people with thee.**
>
> [11] **And thou shalt say, I will go up to the land of unwalled villages; I will go to them that are at rest, that dwell safely, all of them dwelling without walls, and having neither bars nor gates,**
>
> [12]**To take a spoil, and to take a prey; to turn thine hand upon the desolate places that are now inhabited, and upon the people that are gathered out of the nations, which have gotten cattle and goods, that dwell in the midst of the land.**
>
> [15]**And thou shalt come from thy place out of the north parts, thou, and many people with thee, all of them riding upon horses, a great company, and a mighty army:**
>
> [16]**And thou shalt come up against my people of Israel, as a cloud to cover the land; it shall be in the latter days, and I will bring thee against my land, that the heathen may know me, when I shall be sanctified in thee, O Gog, before their eyes** (Ezekiel. 38:9, 11-12, 15-16).

The Third Seal

Then shall occur the opening of the third seal. This seal denotes economic catastrophe.

> **And I beheld, and lo a black horse; and he that sat on him had a pair of balances in his hand. And I heard a voice in the midst of the four beasts say, A measure of wheat for a penny, and three measures of barley for a penny; and see thou hurt not the oil and the wine** (Revelation. 6:5-6).

The balances in verse 5 indicate a shortage of food. The fact that the rider comes on a black horse emphasizes the extremity of this situation. Throughout the Old and New Testaments food, wine, oils, and gold were always measured, indicating their scarcity. But notice the sixth verse **"a measure of wheat for a penny."** In John's day, the average daily wage was a penny. John, in his vision, sees mankind paying a whole day's wages for one measure (about two pints) of wheat. But look what he says about the luxury items like oils and wine. The luxury items will not be affected. Only the very rich will be able to afford the things we now take for granted.

The Fourth Seal

The opening of the fourth seal reveals to us the casualties of the tribulation thus far.

> **And behold a pale horse: and his name that sat on him was Death, and Hell followed with him. And power was given unto them over the fourth part of the earth, to kill with sword** (the main weapon of John's day) **and with hunger, and with death, and with the beasts of the earth** (Revelation 6:8, parenthetical comment mine).

As the war in the Middle East increases into a worldwide conflict, the Bible tells us that the world population will decrease by the death of a billion and a half people, or about one-fourth of our present population. Millions will be killed directly from actual fighting and exchanges of bombs and missiles. Millions more will starve due to the high prices of food and, as verse 6 indicates, the global food shortage.

Even today, the food situation is becoming a worldwide problem. In the past, with a few exceptions, food production has been able to keep up with population growth. Yet, every year the world produces less food, while the population increases by about 78 million. With the decline in food productivity, some nations are now faced with malnutrition and starvation on a large scale.

The Fifth Seal

The opening of the fifth seal reveals the martyrs of the Tribulation. They are **"under the altar."** These are people who were saved during the Tribulation.

> **And when he had opened the fifth seal, I saw under the altar the souls of them that were slain for the word of God, and for the testimony which they held** (Revelation 6:9).

When the antichrist enters the rebuilt temple and proclaims himself to be God, every man, woman, and child will be required to receive an identification number on their hands or foreheads. This number, which the antichrist will introduce himself, will be required of every person who wishes to purchase goods and services. Without the number it will literally be impossible to buy or sell anything. Those without the **"mark of the beast"** (Revelation 16:2), as it will be called, will be considered rebels to the cause of the antichrist. These are the people who will be saved during the Tribulation and will proclaim allegiance to Christ. It will be these Christians who will experience the most severe persecution of all time. To be a Christian in that day may very well cost a person his life.

In our highly computerized and technological age it is not hard to foresee a system of controlling goods and services through an identification number. We already do it with social security, pin, and driver's license numbers. With these numbers anyone can obtain our address, phone number, occupation, personal background, financial status, and even the color of our eyes. The antichrist will have no problem initiating his identification program because we are already familiar with it.

The Sixth Seal

Now we come to the opening of the sixth seal. Up to this point I'm sure the Apostle John had no problem understanding God's divine revelations. I'm sure he was able to conceive of a government whereby a man has complete authority to rule as he desires. After all, John lived under Roman dictatorship. Nor was it out of his realm of comprehension to understand the possibilities of a world economic breakdown, whereby people would die from hunger in the streets. And surely the Apostle John was familiar with the persecution of Christians. But now, John was about to be shown destruction on a scale so large that even he could hardly comprehend it.

Again, let's consider what this servant of God's experienced. Here we see a man familiar only with spears, bows, and arrows, witnessing a world war using the technology of the twenty-first century. He sees weapons made from materials that have not yet been discovered. He hears sounds that he's never heard before. He witnessed death on such a massive scale that even modern day man finds it hard to imagine. God tells John to **"write the things which thou hast seen"** (Revelation 1:19). God tells him to describe what will happen to mankind in the future. And so, the Apostle John in his primitive knowledge and language begins describing a battle.

And I beheld, when he had opened the sixth seal, and, lo, there was a great earthquake; and the sun became black as sackcloth of hair, and the moon became as blood; And the stars of heaven fell unto the earth, even as a fig tree casteth her untimely figs, when she is shaken of a mighty wind. And the heaven departed as a scroll when it is rolled together; and every mountain and island were moved out of their places (Revelation 6:12-14).

In older days they carried spears—
Didn't have rifles like musketeers,
No pistols, cannons or hand grenades—
Just simple sticks with simple blades.

But John describes a gruesome war,
With weapons so superior,
They destroy a third of all mankind,
More than all the wars combined.

Weapons that shake the very ground
With fire and brimstone all around,
So desolate men will be brought to tears.
John knew God wasn't speaking of spears.

Knives and hooks can't shake the land,
Pollute the air and burn the hand,
Consume the flesh from off the bones,
Crack the earth and melt the stones.

John was confused by this forecast—
After all, he described a nuclear blast.

What we are considering here is astonishing. How could a man 2000 years ago, familiar only with primitive weapons, conceive of such a devastating worldwide battle? Less than a century ago that kind of destruction would have seemed unbelievable. This is what separates a true prophet from our modern day "prophets."

From the beginning of man's history, he's sought peace, but war has ultimately prevailed. Scientists around the world gasped at the discovery of dynamite. Surely, they said, no country would be foolish enough to initiate a war using the destructive and mass-killing capabilities of TNT. With the invention of the automatic weapon, governments agreed that peace was surely inevitable. As the Wright brothers experimented with their flying machine, and Count Zeppelin with his dirigible, mankind was sure that the end of wars was in sight. Men insisted that because each side had obtained these new weapons there would prevail what scientists call a "balance of terror." But men soon realized that as the weapons became more and more evil so did man's capacity to use them.

On the morning of August 6, 1945, as the citizens of Hiroshima, Japan hurried to their jobs a single airplane flew silently across the blue sky. There had on other days been frequent air raid warnings when planes passed over Hiroshima on their way to other targets, so it was not significant to see an enemy plane flying over the city. The all clear siren soon followed. Seconds later there was a flash and an explosion equivalent to 20,000 tons of TNT.

The number of deaths immediately, and over a period of time, were estimated at about 92,000. In his award-winning book, *Death in Life: Survivors of Hiroshima*, Robert Jay Lifton sought out people who lived in and around Hiroshima, and told of their first hand experiences of the atomic bomb

.

He interviewed a history professor who described the explosion that threw him to the ground and caused serious burns to his body.

> And then a ... huge boom ... like the rumbling of distant thunder. At the same time a violent rush of air pressed down my entire body ... I raised my head, facing the center of Hiroshima to the west ... There I

saw an enormous mass of clouds… which spread and climbed rapidly… into sky, then its summit broke open and hung over horizontally. It took the shape of… a monstrous mushroom … Beneath it more and more boiling clouds erupted and unfolded sideways… The shape … the color … the light … were continuously shifting and changing…[50]

An electrician who was working at a railroad junction in Hiroshima when the bomb exploded crawled under a nearby locomotive. He said there was a tremendous boom so loud that it shook the locomotive. The history professor also mentioned there was a loud thundering noise. The point here is that the bomb dropped on Hiroshima is considered a primitive bomb today. We now have bombs and missiles that are measured in terms of millions of tons of TNT[51].

One of the most powerful bombs known to man is the cobalt bomb. By placing a shield of cobalt 59 metal around a hydrogen bomb one can double its destructive capabilities. The cobalt bomb is known to scientists as the "dirty bomb" since its radioactive contamination is significant. The tremendous fallout of such a bomb would undoubtedly shield the sun and the moon from the earth. In Revelation 6:12, John says the **"sun became black … and the moon became as blood."** In chapter 8 we see another description of the effects of the fallout.

> **And the third part of the sun was smitten, and the third part of the moon, and the third part of the stars; so as the third part of them was darkened, and the day shone not for a third part of it, and the night likewise** (Revelation 8:12).

According to the description of the Hiroshima history professor, it is not so far-fetched to think that a nuclear exchange of weapons far more powerful than the Hiroshima bomb could easily hide the sun

---

[50] Lifton, Robert Jay, *Death in Life: Survivors of Hiroshima* (New York, NY: Random House, Inc., 1968) p. 19.

[51] Ibid, p. 23.

and cause the day to become dark. One could compare the effects of the bomb with those afternoon thunderstorms we have in the Midwest when it gets so dark that the streetlights automatically turn on.

In Revelation 6:13, John describes stars falling out of the sky; these are missiles. Again you must remember the Apostle John is describing what looked to him like stars. His vocabulary is limited to first century thinking, and to him the only thing that could possibly fall out of the sky would be a meteorite or shooting star. After the stars fall from heaven something unusual will happen, as John tells us that **"the heaven departed like a scroll when it is rolled together"** (verse 14).

Have you ever wondered what happens during a nuclear explosion? Well, this is what John is describing. As soon as the explosion takes place an intensely hot luminous sphere appears which is called the "fireball." Immediately after it is formed the fireball begins to expand and as it decreases in temperature it rises. It is from this fireball, due to the sudden increase in pressure at the point of the explosion that violent winds originate. These fierce winds cause the major amount of destruction as they rush out in all directions. As the fireball continues to cool (approximately 1 minute), vapors within it begin to condense. The vapors then form a cloud containing debris from the bomb and water vapor which gives it the appearance of an ordinary cloud. A strong updraft is then produced as the winds rush back into the point of the explosion filling the vacuum. This causes materials from the earth to be sucked up into the bomb. This residue will eventually fall back to earth. As soon as the cloud rises to a point where the density of the air is the same it begins to spread out giving it the appearance of a mushroom.

The history professor describes this fantastic spectacle of clouds, smoke, and debris as "unfolding sideways" across the sky. The Apostle John said that it reminded him of the way a scroll rolls and spreads across a table.

John then continues to describe the affects of these massive explosions: **"And every mountain and island were moved out of their places"** (verse 14).

In chapter 8:7 there is another explosion. **"The first angel sounded, and there followed hail and fire mingled with blood, and they were cast upon the earth."**

The word hail is defined as "a falling or showering." I believe that hail in verse 7 is referring to a hail of bombs and missiles. This indicates an exchange of bombs and missiles that pour out of the skies.

When a nominal atomic bomb is detonated at a height of about 2000 feet the fireball we talked about earlier develops with a temperature of 300,000 degrees. On a clear day this ball can attain a brilliance of 100 times that of the sun. The result is an outbreak of fires within a radius of several miles. Referring to Lifton's book, he says that the "Heat was so extreme that metal and stone melted, and human beings were literally incinerated. The area was enveloped by fires fanned by violent fire wind."[52]

Another event takes place in heaven with the sounding of a trumpet. The Apostle John describes the effects of this worldwide battle on the ecology of the earth.

> **And the third part of trees was burnt up, and all green grass was burnt up** (Revelation 8:7).

Can you imagine the famines that will occur when one-third of all grass (wheat, barley, etc.) is destroyed? I recently read of a scientist who said that the plant and animal life in the sea could easily alleviate our world food situation. For thousands of years many countries have relied solely upon the sea for their food supply. But notice what happens.

---

[52]   Ibid, p. 20.

And the second angel sounded, and as it were a great mountain burning with fire was cast into the sea; and the third part of the sea became blood; And the third part of the creatures which were in the sea, and had life, died; and the third part of the ships were destroyed (Revelation 8:8-9).

In verse 8 the phrase **"As it were a great mountain burning with fire."** The key words are *as it were,* which translate to mean *as if* or "looks like." Here John witnesses a hail of missiles and bombs falling into the seas killing a third of all sea life. The purpose of this is explained in the second half of verse 9 when it says, **"The third part of ships were destroyed."** The death of one third of all life in the sea is due to the bombing of major seaports around the world. This is also probably the result of a great naval battle that contributes to the food shortage by destroying merchant ships. In verse 12 the rivers and lakes around the world are also affected by this great atomic holocaust.

And the fourth angel sounded, and the third part of the sun was smitten, and the third part of the moon, and the third part of the stars; so as the third part of them were darkened, and the day shone not for a third part of it, and the night likewise (Revelation 8:12).

John Hersey, a Pulitzer Prize winning author, also went to Japan and interviewed a woman who, with her children, survived the catastrophic event. He wrote, "Mrs. Nakamura took the children out into the street. They had nothing on but their underpants,... The children were silent, except for the five year-old, Myeko, who kept asking the question, 'Why is it night already?'" (The bomb exploded at 8:00 a.m.).[53]

Once again we see the affects of the air pollution following a nuclear explosion. The sunlight around the earth is reduced by one

---

[53]   http://www.american-buddha.com/lit/hiroshima.2.html

third. This will definitely have a serious effect on the world food situation. The portions of wheat and other crops that were not directly destroyed during the fighting will be affected because of the reduction of sunlight, and thus the process of photosynthesis, which is vital to the survival of plant life on earth, will be drastically slowed down.

And the first [angel] went, and poured out his vial upon the earth; and there fell a noisome and grievous sore upon the men which has the mark of the beast (Revelation 16:2).

Jesus said that in the last days there would be pestilence in epidemic proportions. The above verse describes a sore that will strike more terror in the hearts of man than cancer does today. In my studies of the Hiroshima bomb it was almost inevitable that those who lived within a certain distance from the point of the explosion and were not killed by the initial blast were later stricken with a peculiar disease. Doctors did not know what it was nor could they prescribe an effective treatment. The symptoms were: loss of hair, nausea, vomiting, fever, and the appearance of spots under the skin. Finally, accompanied by hemorrhaging of the mouth, rectum, and gums, sores appeared on the skin. It was dubbed the "A-bomb disease."

The atomic bomb that was dropped on Hiroshima was nicknamed "Little Boy," which is exactly what it was compared to the powerful weapons of today. Yet, I find it hard to imagine the potential of these bombs when I read about the killing and maiming ability of the "Little Boy." Here are a few testimonies from those survivors who were interviewed by Robert Lifton.

The history professor: "A blinding ... flash cut sharply across the sky... I threw myself to the ground ... in a reflex movement ... the skin over my body felt a burning heat."

Shopkeeper's assistant: "There was a noise and I felt a great heat—even in the house."

A grocer: "The appearance of people was … well, they all had skin blackened by burns … they had no hair … their skin, not only on their hands, but on their faces and bodies too—hung down."[54]

During John Hersey's interviews, he talked with a priest who went to fetch drinking water for those who could not go for themselves. The priest describes a group of soldiers he found in a clump of bushes. "Their faces were wholly burned, their eye sockets were hollow, and the fluid from their melted eyes had run down their checks. Their mouths were mere swollen, pus-covered wounds." The prophet Zechariah prophesied of this kind of event when he said:

Their flesh shall consume away while they stand upon their feet, and their eyes shall consume away in their holes, and their tongue shall consume away in the mouth (Zechariah 14:12).

Earlier generations had the ability to effect history. Today we literally have the power to end it. Not until this day of atomic bombs has mankind developed weapons that are able to melt the flesh from bones before the body has time to hit the ground. For the first time mankind has at his command the ability to do what scientists call "overkill." Overkill is the destructive ability to kill the entire population of our planet many times over.

During the early 1960s, Nikita Khrushchev announced the "Doomsday Bomb," which was equivalent to 100 megatons or 100 million tons of TNT. It is hard to visualize the destruction experienced by the first atomic bomb, but to comprehend the ability of a 100 megaton bomb is unimaginable. Dropping a 100 megaton bomb would be the same as bombing Hiroshima every day with the same destructive force as the "Little Boy" for thirteen years.

---

[54]   Lifton, Robert Jay, *Death in Life: Survivors of Hiroshima* (New York, NY: Random House, Inc., 1968.

It would be sheer fantasy to think that nations would not use the weapons of the nuclear age. Whether through accident, madness, or actual declaration of war, leaders and scientists remind us that nuclear war is becoming inevitable. After all, the bomb was used in the past, so what makes us believe that it will not be used in the future? Can we believe that there could not be another maniac like Hitler? What about an accidental war?

The Seventh Seal

The seventh seal introduces the next part of John's vision, the Seven Trumpets followed by the Seven Bowls of Wrath.

> **And when he had opened the seventh seal, there was silence in heaven about the space of half an hour** (Revelation 8:1).

> **And I heard a great voice out of the temple saying to the seven angels, Go your ways, and pour out the vials of the wrath of God upon the earth** (Revelation 16:1).

The seven seals (Revelation 6), seven trumpets (Revelation 8-9), and seven vials (bowls) of wrath (Revelation 15-16) are three judgment series and must be understood according to their chronological order. The three judgments are redemptive and create a global crisis that result in many being saved. They are progressive in that they increase in intensity as each series of judgments is released. The seal judgments are surpassed in their intensity by the trumpet judgments, which are then surpassed in intensity by the vials of wrath.

CHAPTER TEN
They Will Not Repent

A chain of events will begin as God counts off the seven years of the Tribulation. A series of judgments will take place beginning with the opening of the first of the seven seals. Each seal initiates a major worldwide event. The judgment of the Seven Seals will be followed by the judgments of the Seven Trumpets and then the Seven Bowls of Wrath. Shockingly, the nations will not repent and turn to God.

Overview of the Seals

- The rise to power of the antichrist. He is depicted as a conqueror on a white horse. He will bring a false peace to a chaotic world (Revelation 6:1-2).
- The peace and harmony in the world will be shattered as the second seal is broken and a rider on a red horse brings war against the state of Israel (6:3-4).
- Food and the necessities of life will become scarce with the opening of the third seal (6:5-6).
- The fourth seal will reveal casualties as a result of famines, epidemics, and civil violence (6:7-8).
- Seal number five will spark the beginning of Christian persecution such as the world has never known (6:9-11).
- The sixth seal is opened. After years of wondering if a nuclear war would someday be a reality, man's answer will come as a deluge of bombs and missiles fall from the sky (6:12-17).
- The seventh and last seal contains all the remaining divine judgments of the trumpets and bowls/vials (8:1-5).

The Seven Trumpets

- The focus of the first four trumpets (Revelation 8:6-13) is on the earth's environment, trees, rivers, and atmosphere (8:6-13).

- The fifth trumpet's focus will shift from the physical realm (the earth) to the spiritual realm. A star will fall from heaven but it will not be an inanimate piece of matter but an angelic being: the devil (Isaiah 14:12-15; Luke 10:18). Satan and his demons will plague the earth, inflicting pain on those who do not have the seal of God on their forehead (9:1-12).
- The sixth trumpet (9:13-21) will herald another even more severe demonic attack on mankind that will bring death (9:13-21).
- The sounding of the seventh trumpet will announce the bowls/vials of wrath. It sets in motion the final sequence of events that will lead to the return of Jesus Christ.

The Seven Vials

At the prospect of Christ's return and the inevitable establishment His kingdom draws near, the twenty-four elders begin to worship God. The impenitent nations will become more defiant at the prospect of Christ's coming kingdom (Revelation 11:15-19).

- The first bowl (vial) will bring a plague of sores that will torment all unbelievers (16:2).
- The angel will pour out the second bowl into the seas causing the waters to become putrid and unable to sustain life. (16:3).
- The third bowl judgment will cause the rivers and all fresh water on earth to become undrinkable and uninhabitable (16:4-7).
- When the fourth angel pours out his bowl, the sun will increase its intensity. The temperature on earth will rise and those people with the mark of the beast will be scorched by fierce heat (16:8-9).
- Darkness will engulf the entire earth as the fifth angel pours out his bowl (10-11).
- The river Euphrates will dry up when the sixth bowl is emptied. This judgment prepares a way for the kings of the east to march across the dried riverbed and into a place called Har-Magedon. There they will be defeated by God (16:12-16).

- The seventh bowl is the final outpouring of God's wrath. It will have devastating effects on the earth's atmosphere and the earth itself (16:17-21).

> **And the kings of the earth, and the great men, and the rich men, and the chief captains, and the mighty men, and every bondman, and every free man, hid themselves in the dens and in the rocks of the mountains; and said to the mountains and rocks, Fall on us, and hide us from the face of him that sitteth on the throne, and from the wrath of the Lamb: For the great day of his wrath is come; and who shall be able to stand?** (Revelation. 6:15-17).

In these final verses we see people fleeing from the turbulent cities to the temporary safety of the hills and mountains. The war becomes more intense as more bombs and missiles destroy cities and kill millions of people. As horrible as these events are, the remaining inhabitants of earth refuse to turn to God.

> **And the rest of the men which were not killed by these plagues yet repented not of the works of their hands, that they should not worship devils, and idols of gold, and silver, and brass, and stone, and of wood: which neither can see, nor hear, nor walk: Neither repented they of their murders, nor of their sorceries, nor of their fornication, nor of their thefts.** (Revelation 9:20-21).

Taking a closer look at these verses we see the five big sins of the Tribulation period: the worshiping of devils, (hardly a possibility to be disregarded in an age where high schools and universities across the country offer courses on the subject), murders; sorceries (sorcery comes from the Greek word pharmakia, which means pharmacy, and in this context refers to drug-related occult activities); fornication (immorality); and theft.

The people of the earth will become more resistant toward God and curse Him.

> **And men were scorched with great heat, and blasphemed the name of God, which hath power over these plagues: and they repented not to give him glory ... And blasphemed the God of heaven because of their pains and their sores, and repented not of their deeds** (Revelation 16:9, 11).

A Place Called Armageddon

> **And he gathered them together into a place called in the Hebrew tongue Armageddon. And the seventh angel poured out his vial into the air; and there came a great voice out of the temple of heaven, from the throne, saying, "It is done" ... and there was a great earthquake, such as was not since men were upon the earth ... And every island fled away and the mountains were not found ... and men blasphemed God** (Revelation 16:16-18, 20-21).

This is indeed a sad thing for the Apostle John to have witnessed. Great cities such as New York, London, Tokyo, Moscow, Rome and Paris are nothing but smoldering ashes. The world would look as one would expect the "end of the world" to look. John prophesied this event when he said in Revelation 16:19 **"And the cities of the nations fell."**

> **Every man's sword shall be against his brother. And I will plead against him with pestilence and with blood; and I will rain upon him, and upon his bands, and upon the many people that are with him, an over flowing rain, and great hailstones, fire, and brimstone. Thus will I magnify myself, and sanctify**

myself; and I will be known in the eyes of many nations, and they shall know that I am the Lord (Ezekiel 38:21-23).

Through the horrors of Armageddon, God will exalt Himself in the eyes of all mankind. In those days, atheists, worshipers of false gods, will acknowledge the true and perfect God who created them. But instead of falling to their knees and repenting of their sins, the Bible says that they will blaspheme and curse the name of God.

As the Armageddon campaign swiftly escalates, the prophet Ezekiel describes the destruction of Russia and her allies. Just as the Jewish people recognized that God's hand was in the mysterious disappearance of millions of Christians before the Tribulation, they will also recognize God's divine intervention as the odds turn in their favor. The Jewish people will be supernaturally saved from the Antichrist and his armies. (This should not be so hard to believe since history records many wars and battles in which the Hebrew race had been totally outnumbered but miraculously recovered and won the battle.) Ezekiel said,

And I will send a fire on Magog, and among them that dwell carelessly in the isles: and they shall know that I am the Lord. So will I make my holy name known in the midst of my people Israel; and I will not let them pollute my holy name any more: and the heathen shall know that I am the Lord, the Holy One in Israel. Behold, it is come, and it is done, saith the Lord God; this is the day whereof I have spoken (Ezekiel 39:6-8).

Again we see that God exalts Himself to the Jewish people through the destruction of Magog's invading forces. It is at that time that the prophet Zachariah (13:8-9) predicts that one third of all the Jews will repent and be converted to Christ. While these are miraculously preserved, the remainder will be killed.

The nations of the world are prepared for war. Military arsenals are stocked with enough firepower to destroy our planet's population many times over. Today, men vainly seek peace and at the same time reject the only hope for peace, Jesus Christ.

The word peace is mentioned over 400 times throughout the Bible. It is used mostly in figures of speech: "peace be with you," or "he went in peace." Never do we find the word peace apart from Christ used to describe a future of complete world harmony. In Isaiah 9:6, Jesus Christ is described as, among other things, the **"Prince of Peace."**

One out of every twenty-five verses in the New Testament is related to the second coming of Jesus. In the Old Testament there are over 300 prophecies relating to the coming of the Messiah, all of which have been literally fulfilled. The ironic fact about the Old Testament prophecies concerning Jesus' first coming is that many of those verses also tell of his return. Over 500 prophecies of Christ's return are found in the Old Testament, yet people around the world scoff at Jesus' promise: **"I go to prepare a place for you. And if I go and prepare a place for you, I will come again, and receive you unto myself; that where I am, there ye may be also"** (John 14:2b-3). They insist that the world will continue just as it is now. The Apostle Peter tells us that attitude is a sign that His coming is near (2 Peter 3:3, 4).

CHAPTER ELEVEN
The Rider on the White Horse

And I saw heaven opened, and behold a white horse; and he that sat upon him was called Faithful and True, and in righteousness he doth judge and make war. His eyes were as a flame of fire, and on his head were many crowns; and he had a name written, that no man knew, but he himself. And he was clothed with a vesture dipped in blood: and his name is called The Word of God. And the armies which were in heaven followed him upon white horses, clothed in fine linen, white and clean. And out of his mouth goeth a sharp sword, that with it he should smite the nations: and he shall rule them with a rod of iron: and he treadeth the winepress of the fierceness and wrath of Almighty God. And he hath on his vesture and on his thigh a name written, KING OF KINGS, AND LORD OF LORDS (Revelation 19:11-16).

The Apostle John was closer to the Lord Jesus than all the other Apostles. His affection for his Savior was seen often and none as obvious as when he leaned his head upon Christ in the upper room. John knew more than all the others of Christ's painful beatings. He had seen his Lord on that terrible and agonizing night at Gethsemane. In Herod's Palace and Pilate's Hall, John saw Him after He had been beaten and scourged. He stood near the cross and saw his Lord in the pain and agony of crucifixion. The sufferings of John's blessed Savior would forever be etched in his mind.

John saw Jesus Christ as a lone Warrior fighting a great battle. He had no troops that followed Him. All of His disciples fled. He said by the prophet Isaiah, **"I have trodden the winepress alone; and**

of the people there was none with me" (Isaiah 63:3). This Soldier wore no glittering armor, rode no gallant steed, but walked into battle wearing sandals and a robe. His clothing was red with His own blood, and His face was smeared with gory sweat. He was a solitary soldier and did not appear to be a threat to His enemies. He fought against sin and death and He fell. His enemies rejoiced at His death. Then He arose from out of the tomb and ascended into heaven.

On the Island of Patmos, John saw Jesus as he had never seen Him before. He saw the same Warrior, but He was different. It was the same battle between good and evil, truth and error, Christ and Satan, but from God's point of view. Through John's eyes and his book of the Revelation we look down on the battle from a heavenly perspective.

Heaven's door opens and **"behold a white horse"** (Revelation 19:11). The Rider is Jesus Christ. On the earth He walked; He was a foot-soldier. He trudged through the dust and mire. He walked from city to city. He would often grow weary and have need of rest. But now He rides on a gallant horse charging into the enemy's camp. We grieved as we read how He groveled beneath the olive trees in Gethsemane, but now we are glad, for He comes riding a white horse. He comes to fight against His enemies, who are our enemies. He is no fainting foot-soldier any longer, but a glorious Conqueror. He once gave Himself to be hung on a cross in shame, but now He is mounted on a white horse, which signifies this victory, and He rules the heavens and the earth.

John described the character of the Rider: **"He that sat upon him was called Faithful and True"** He has always been faithful and true to His promises. Has He ever failed, deceived or forgotten you? The work of saving you; has He accomplished that work? He did not draw back from the cross. He said He would stand in your place and receive the wrath for your sin and He did. He has been truthful even to the most depraved and wicked devil. To their regret, Jesus Christ will keep His promise to bring judgment upon them. Jesus said He will bind Satan for a thousand years and He will.

John also sees another characteristic of Jesus Christ: **"In righteousness he doth judge and make war."** This can only be said of Him. War is as filled with deceit and lies as it is bloody. Leaders of nations deliberate about peace and formulate their treaties and soon break them. Deception is the normal way of war. Jesus wages war against His enemies speaking honestly and truthfully. He does not mince words. He means what He says and says what He means. If He speaks about judgment, you can be sure that judgment will come and it will be terrible.

"His eyes were as a flame of fire" (19:12), therefore John must look away. Our Lord's eyes were often red and filled with tears. He was **"A man of sorrows, and acquainted with grief"** (Isaiah 53:3). Now His eyes are bright and dazzling, like two balls of fire. Jesus Christ sees all things. Nothing is hidden from His sight. There is no thought or motive, no unbelief or hypocrisy, no deceit that His eyes cannot penetrate and discern. His eyes understand all the plots and schemes of His enemies. He knows all of their ways and will foil all of their efforts.

It was natural that John's glance should move from Christ's eyes to the top of His head. **"And on his head were many crowns; and he had a name written, that no man knew, but he himself"** (Revelation 19:12). What an amazing contrast must have passed through John's mind. Where there was once a crown of thorns there is now a crown adorned with precious jewels. From earthly briars and sharp edges, there is now gold and silver. Once Christ wore a crown of mockery, derision and contempt; He now wears a crown of heavenly nobility. And there are many crowns. There is the crown of grace; grace flows from His hands. There is the crown of the Church; He is the head of the Church. There are crowns from those He has saved.

Contemplate the One who rides in on the white horse and notice **"He was clothed with a vesture dipped in blood: and his name is called The Word of God"** (19:13). Our Lord Jesus Christ, who alone can atone for sin, is wearing the bloody garments of sacrifice. That He bled for us is the most wonderful thought we have of our Messiah. His life was glorious, but His death transcended it a thousand times. As the blood is the life so is His blood to us life eternal. It is our hope and peace. Our Savior rides in on a white horse, but He still wears the bloody robe in which He won our redemption.

John sees Christ's followers: **"And the armies which were in heaven followed him upon white horses, clothed in fine linen, white and clean"** (19:14). On earth He had only a handful of followers and in the end they abandoned Him. Now Christ has a great following; He has armies—not one, but many. They are the countless number of souls saved out of every tribe and tongue and people and nation. They are all on white horses, but they do not carry weapons; there is not a sword or pistol among them. They are clothed in white linen. What a strange army, but this is how they conquer their enemies. Holiness and righteousness are their weapons.

John does see a single weapon, **"And out of his mouth goeth a sharp sword, that with it he should smite the nations"** (19:15). Only One carries a sword, and the sword is in Christ's mouth—a strange place to carry a weapon. The sword is the Gospel and with it He smites the nations. However, if they will not believe the Gospel, then John says, **"He shall rule them with a rod of iron."** And if they reject Him, He will subdue His enemies in a most dreadful manner. **"And he treadeth the winepress of the fierceness and wrath of Almighty God"** He will crush them as clusters of grapes in a winepress. His mercy will be gone. He will be fierce and terrible.

I pray that, on that day, you too will have a white horse with which to follow Jesus Christ. You cannot follow Him there unless you first are following Him here. You must put on the white linen of salvation now. Here is your garment: the righteousness of Jesus Christ.

CHAPTER TWELVE
Christ's Return

For hundreds of years people have scoffed at Christ's promise that He will return. Some professing Christians do not believe that Christ will literally return to earth. They theorize that when Christ said He would return He meant it in a spiritual sense; that He would return to spiritually possess individuals when they accepted Him as their Savior. They believe that if you are a Christian, having submitted yourself to Jesus as your Lord and Savior, then you have experienced "the second coming." Others insist that the second coming is when a person dies and Jesus returns to earth for their soul. Yet there is nothing in the Bible to support this kind of teaching.

> **And when he had spoken these things, while they beheld, he was taken up; and a cloud received him out of their sight. And while they looked steadfastly toward heaven as he went up, behold, two men stood by them in white apparel ...** (Acts 1:9-10).

As the disciples stood anxiously waiting for Jesus to speak again, they witnessed a more spectacular event than the launching of the space shuttle at Cape Canaveral, Florida. Without the aid of any highly technical apparatus, Jesus defied the law of gravity and ascended into the sky. As the disciples watched, amazed, two angels appeared in the form of men and said:

> **Ye men of Galilee, why stand ye gazing up into heaven? This same Jesus, which is taken up from you into heaven, shall so come in like manner as ye have seen him go into heaven** (Acts 1:11).

The key words in this verse are *in like manner,* which mean in exactly the same way. Jesus Christ literally left the earth, and the disciples saw Him go. Christ promised to return in the same way. One out of every twenty-five verses in the New Testament reminds us of His second coming.

In the life story of our Lord Jesus Christ there are four events that shine like jewels: His birth, death, resurrection and ascension into heaven. We could not dispense with any of these four events. We are amazed at how He humbled Himself and was born of a young woman. In this we have a common brotherhood and humanity. Then Jesus suffered and died a horrible death; a wonder we can barely comprehend. We are astounded and awed at just how far He stooped to make our redemption possible. The manger and the cross are the divine seals of God's stupendous love. What condescension!   Jesus' resurrection from the dead is the guarantee of our justification and eternal life. Jesus said **"Because I live ye shall live also"** (John 14:19). Jesus' ascension is no less wonderful than His resurrection.

And there is a fifth. It is our Lord's second coming. Jesus Christ ascended and will again descend. No history is mentioned in Acts 1:11 between Christ's ascending and descending However, there is a rich history, but it lies in a valley between two magnificent mountains; Christ's going up into heaven and Christ's coming back. The previous four events point to this one event. Had Jesus not come the first time as a little child in lowliness and humility, He could not come a second time riding a white horse in glory and majesty (Revelation 19:11).

Zechariah records another startling prophecy concerning Christ's return to the earth:

> **Then shall the Lord go forth, and fight against those nations, as when he fought in the day of battle. And his feet shall stand in that day upon the mount of Olives, which is before Jerusalem on the east, and the mount of Olives shall cleave in the midst thereof toward the east and toward the west, and there shall be a very great valley; and half of the mountain shall**

remove toward the north, and half of it toward the south. And ye shall flee to the valley of the mountains … and the Lord my God shall come, and all the saints with thee (Zechariah 14:3-5).

In Acts 1:12, after Jesus ascended into heaven, the disciples returned from the Mount of Olives and went back to Jerusalem. Zechariah said that **"his feet shall stand in that day upon the mount of Olives."** Jesus not only returns physically and visibly, but as the Bible tells us, He returns to the exact spot from which He ascended.

His return is at the height of a great battle between the Antichrist and the armies of Gog, which have drawn the largest ground forces ever assembled. Remember, this will include the vast Chinese army as well as the Arab-African forces. Although the Bible does not mention the United States, it appears that we shall be allied with the European countries headed by the Antichrist. This great battle, which the Bible calls Armageddon, will extend 200 miles. And the description of it in Revelation 14:20 assures us that this will be the goriest fight that man has ever initiated.

The word Armageddon comes from the Greek word Har-Megiddo which is the name of an ancient city approximately fifty miles north of Jerusalem. Founded about 3500 B.C., Megiddo has been the site of many important battles. Napoleon won a battle there against the Turks in 1799. It was the site of a decisive battle at the end of World War 1 in which the British surrounded the Turkish forces.

Zechariah tells us that the moment Jesus' foot touches down on the mountain the mountain will split from east to west causing a great valley. It is at that time that the Jewish people will realize that Jesus Christ is the Messiah. They will flee into this great chasm. Is this a coincidence? Hardly. A geographical fault has been discovered running from east to west through the Mount of Olives. "The geological institute in Tel Aviv discovered a major fault line running right through the Mount of Olives. It takes a line from the Mount Olives over to the

Kidron valley all the way into the valley of Hinnom. The fault line follows the Kidron Brook which empties into the Dead Sea.[55]

It is Jesus' foot that will trigger this earthquake!

> **And I saw heaven open, and behold a white horse; and he that sat upon him was called Faithful and True, and in righteousness he doth judge and make war. His eyes were as a flame of fire, and on his head were many crowns; and he had a name written, that no man knew, but he himself. And he was clothed with a vesture dipped in blood: and his name is called The Word of God** (Revelation 19:11-13).

As the fighting escalates, mankind finds himself on the brink of annihilation. The scene will be transformed instantly as Jesus Himself appears, descending from heaven mounted on a white horse. The white horse will emphasize His intentions to conquer the world. It will be a startling and paramount entrance unlike His first coming as a humble and submissive servant. His grandeur and unexpected appearance will no doubt cause the fighting to cease. Jesus describes this startling event:

> **For as the lightening cometh out of the east, and shineth even unto the west; so shall also the coming of the Son of Man be. And then shall appear the sign of the Son of Man in heaven: and then shall all the tribes of the earth mourn, and they shall see the Son of Man coming in the clouds of heaven with power and great glory** (Matthew 24:27, 30).

Notice that it says that He comes **"in the clouds of heaven."** Several times throughout the Bible the word cloud is mentioned. These are not literal clouds but, as Hebrew 12:1 implies, are clouds of **"witnesses."** They are the Christians who were caught up in the rapture

---

55   http://www.abbaswatchman.com/PAGE%2023%20DEAD%20SEA%20 PAGE%202.htm

prior to the Tribulation. Zechariah prophesied of Christ returning with the "saints." Over sixty times in the New Testament the word saint refers to the true believers of Jesus Christ. Several of the New Testament books open with the author addressing the church members as "saints."

In a matter of a few seconds after Christ appears in this great exhibition of power and glory, the people of the earth will realize their fate. It will be a very tragic scene as the inhabitants of the earth uncontrollably mourn the fact that Jesus is indeed the Son of God.

And all kindreds of the earth shall wail because of him (Revelation 1:7).

In Revelation 19:11, Christ is called **"Faithful and True."** This denotes Christ's loyalty to His promises. His flaming eyes symbolize His vengeance while the crowns tell us that He is indeed **"King of Kings."** The sword in Christ's mouth is a symbol that He comes to destroy those who oppose Him.

The beast, and the kings of the earth, and their armies, gather together to make war against him that sat on the horse (Revelation 19:19).

It is indeed an ironic situation that after thousands of years of fighting with one another, the people of the world finally form an alliance. The hardening of men's hearts reaches its peak as they attempt to overthrow the Son of God. Man turns his guns and missiles toward Jesus Christ.

And the remnant were slain with the sword of him that sat upon the horse (Revelation 19:21).

For God so loved the world, that he gave his only begotten Son, that whosoever believeth in him should not perish, but have everlasting life (John 3:16).

Conclusion
What Should We Do Until Our Lord Returns?

And he that sat upon the throne said, Behold, I make all things new. And he said unto me; Write: for these words are true and faithful (Revelation 21:5).

When God first made the world it was perfect. It was a beautiful garden, full of everything that was lovely, happy and holy. And from the beginning, it was God's desire to have a relationship with mankind. We can only imagine a world where every person loved God, every house was a temple and there was no sorrow or death. What a wonderful and blessed world this would have been had the first creation continued as God had made it. But the serpent came and by his craftiness and deceit spoiled it all. It has become a horribly immoral and ungodly place. Demons themselves could not be worse than men left to their own desires and passions; not even wolves tear one another to pieces as men do. One would think that God would destroy it immediately, never to remake it again. He has always known that mankind could never make a better world, and from the beginning it has been His objective and intention to make the world entirely new.

That process of making all things new began with the making of a new covenant. And, by the work of the Holy Spirit, God has continued to make men new under that new covenant. These people make up the Church, the Bride of Christ, and ultimately, even the earth itself will be made new. From east to west and from north to south, there will be a new world. There will be no injustice, no envying, no anger, no oppression, because all men will have new hearts. It will be a world of righteousness where Christ reigns over all. It will be a happy day, when the lion will lay down with the lamb and men will **"beat their swords into plowshares, and their spears into pruninghooks: nation shall not lift up sword against nation, neither shall they**

learn war any more" (Isaiah 2:4). The day will come when this world will be just as it was originally. Jesus will make a new heaven and new earth. The old things will pass away and all things will be made new. The ancient prophecy, **"Behold, I make all things new,"** will be fulfilled to the very letter. Once again, God will dwell among men.

In fact, the great plan of redemption promises Christ's return. Among His last words, Jesus said, **"Surely I come quickly"** (Revelation 22:20). He has given us His word and that is our reason for expecting Him. Jesus Christ has come once and He will come again. He came once as a sin-offering and will come again to claim the inheritance He purchased with His own blood (John 14:3) He came once and the serpent bruised His heel and He will come again to break the serpent's head (Genesis 3:15). He will come to glorify the saints that were, like Himself, despised and rejected of men (John 15:20). The whole plan of redemption cannot be perfected without the second coming of the Lord Jesus Christ.

But essential to the process of making all things new is the coming Judgment of Christ. Before He goes about the work of making a new heaven and a new earth, the old must be done away with. And in order to do this we're told, in Revelation 20:11-15, that the Lord Jesus Christ will judge all the peoples of the earth with absolute sovereignty. And while there are various aspects to this judgment, one thing is abundantly clear: *all will face Christ*. All will give an account of what they have done in this life.

For those who've trusted in Christ for salvation—who have, by grace through faith, repented of their sins, lived lives of absolute surrender to the Lordship of Christ, and pursued obedience to Him in all that His Word demands (John 14:15, 21-24 and 15:1-14; Ephesians 2:8, 9; Philippians 2:12-13)—this judgment will be a time of rejoicing, not because they've achieved God's holy standard of perfection, but because they have trusted in the sacrifice of Christ on their behalf, to atone for their sins and justify them before the Father (Romans 3:21-26; Ephesians 1:7-14). It is this coming judgment, and the reward of eternity in heaven with Christ, that provides believers with hope and motivation and joy that results in obedient living now, in lives that are productive for Christ and prepared for what is to come (John 15:1-8; Romans 5:20-6:22; Philippians 2:12-13). Those who have entrusted themselves to the God of the universe, to the only Lord and Savior Jesus Christ, will not face their Judge with the terror of eternal punishment, but with the joy of eternal communion with God and with the saints (Matthew 25:31-46; John 6:40, 47; Romans 6:22-23; Ephesians 2:4-7). They will stand before Him acquitted, innocent, officially declared, "Not guilty!"

But for those who don't know Christ, who live in either outright rebellion against Him or apathetic complacency toward Him (Matthew 11:20-24; 23:1-36; 24:36-51; 25:14-46), the coming judgment holds an entirely different meaning. On that day, despite claims of faith and good works, multitudes will be told, **"I never knew you: depart from me"** (Matthew 7:23). While those who have known Christ find that their names are written in the Lamb's Book of Life, those who've rejected Him will learn with absolute certainty that their names are not found there (Revelation 13:5, 8; 20:11-15), and because of this they will face with unspeakable terror the torments of hell (Matthew 7:21; John 15:6; 2 Thessalonians 1:8, 9; Revelation 21:8). Despite good deeds and good intentions, all will bow before Him, declaring that He alone is Lord (Matthew 7:21-23; Philippians 2:8-11). Regardless of the intensity with which they've held to their beliefs, those who've trusted in anything or anyone other than Jesus Christ will find that their lives were devoted to lies, for it will become absolutely clear that there is only one Savior, the Lord Jesus Christ.

But there is hope. There's hope in the Gospel of Jesus Christ. If you hold this book in your hands, then you still have the opportunity to turn to Christ for salvation. While rejecting Him will bring certain punishment in hell, embracing Him will bring certain salvation, certain forgiveness, certain hope of eternity in heaven with Christ (John 6:40; Romans 10:9-13; Ephesians 1:7). Believe that He alone can save you (Acts 4:12; Romans 10:9-13). Understand that your sins have separated you from a holy and just God (Romans 3:23; Ephesians 2:1-3). Turn to Him in faith (Romans 10:9, 10). Fall on your face before Him in humble repentance (Mark 1:15), and find salvation in Him!

The message of this book is urgent. The times in which we live demand that we be certain of our salvation. They demand that we heed the warnings of Scripture and that we do all we can to ensure that we're prepared for what is to come. In light of what we've considered in this book, we must ask ourselves, "How are we to respond to the urgency of these times? In what ways do we prepare ourselves? What should we *do* until our Lord returns to make all things new?"

Jesus answered those very questions long ago:

Blessed are those servants, whom the lord when he cometh shall find watching: verily I say unto you, that he shall gird himself, and make them to sit down to meat, and will come forth and serve them. And if he shall come in the second watch, or come in the third watch, and find them so, blessed are those servants (Luke 12:37, 38).

Jesus stated over and over that we are to watch for His coming, so that when He comes we will be ready. Our Lord's coming will be at an hour when we are not aware (Luke 12:46), and because of that we are to stand in expectation that He may come in a minute or in an hour. Jesus Himself said that He will come in His own time, **"in such an hour as ye think not the Son of man cometh"** (Matthew 24:44). That coming may be tomorrow or it may be next year, but because we do not know when it will be, we must always live as if He were coming today! He *will* come; His return is imminent. We must be certain of our salvation and certain that we're watching in expectation. Let this be our comfort and joy and motivation: He may come today!

When Jesus comes let Him also not find us idle: **"Let your loins be girded about, and your lights burning"** (Luke 12:35). The long robes worn in Jesus' day had a tendency to get in the way, and if a man had work to do he would tuck his robe up under his girdle or belt; it would be equivalent to our saying "roll up your shirtsleeves" and get to work. The story is told of a farmer who had been working in the fields on a hot July day. His pastor stopped by his home to pay him a visit. Embarrassed by his sweaty, dirty clothes he said, "I hope Jesus doesn't return with me looking so grimy and filthy." His pastor answered, "This is the way our Lord would like to see you, busy at work." May Jesus come and find us, not napping on the sofa, but doing our duty. May He find us watching and, at the same time, engaged in whatever vocation God has called us to, out of love for Christ. **"Whatsoever ye do, do all to the glory of God"** (1 Corinthians 10:31). This is the way we wait for the Lord's return.

Another important part of watching for the return of our Lord Jesus Christ is that we not to be obsessed with worldly things. Jesus said, **"take no thought of your life, what ye shall eat; neither for the body, what ye shall put on. The life is more than meat, and the body is more than raiment"** (Luke 12:22-23). We are not to live selfish and fleshly lives, asking what we shall eat and drink, and how can we store up more wealth (Luke 12:15-21, 29-34). Instead, our attention should be focused on the Kingdom of God; our eyes should be fixed on Christ. We have immortal souls and we belong to God; therefore, we must be watching for our Savior's return to take us to the home He has prepared for us (John 14:1-4). Let us not be earth-bound, but as the apostle Paul admonished us, **"Set your affection on things above, not on things on the earth. For ye are dead, and your life is hid with Christ in God"** (Colossians 3:2, 3).

In order for us to set our affections on things above and not be consumed with the things of this world, we must be abiding in Christ (John 15:11). And that requires that we be in the Scriptures, reading them, meditating upon them and obeying them, so that we can conform our lives more and more to His will. It also means that we must be prayerful, so that our wills are bent toward His and we're taught to rely upon Him alone (Hebrews 4:14-16). It also means that we will be growing spiritually, becoming less and less sinful and more and more like Jesus, actively producing the fruits of repentance and obedience to the Lord in our thoughts and speech and behavior (Ephesians 4:20-24). And as Hebrews 10:23, 24 exhorts us, we must not neglect assembling with the body of believers, the church, for He has ordained the church for our equipping and edification and exhortation (Ephesians 4:11-16), something we're especially needful of as we get closer and closer to His returning.

While we are watching for His return, we must also make our light shine among our neighbors and friends. Is our conduct and character pleasing to Christ, demonstrating to those around us that we have new life in Him? Are we telling others how they too may have eternal life? We are not to be like some who hide their light under a bushel basket; we must stand with our lamps trimmed, brightly burning, and waiting for the return of our Lord and Savior (Matthew 5:14-16). As others see our faithful confidence and trust in God during the urgency of these times, we will make them thirst for what we have. We must be about those things which last for eternity: the Word of God and the souls of men.

Finally, we will find great blessing in our watchfulness: **"Blessed are those servants, whom the lord when he cometh shall find watching"** (Luke 12:37). When we watch, always anticipating His return, we are blessed even before He comes. Watching has a way of detaching us from the cares of the world. We are able to be poor and be happy; we are able to be rich and not be worldly; we are able to be sick and not be sorrowful; and so on. Untold blessings are wrapped up in the hope of Christ's return. Keep waiting, working, watching, and when Christ returns we will enter into even greater blessings!

Benediction

At the end of the Book of Revelation, John closes with a benediction: **"The grace of our Lord Jesus Christ be with you all. Amen."** Jesus Christ is everywhere throughout John's Book of Revelation. The first verse declares the precious name of Jesus Christ and the last verse repeats it. He is the sum and substance and glory of every vision John saw on the island of Patmos. John could not conclude the book without drawing attention to that name which was dearest to him: Jesus Christ. And as John lays aside his pen, he concludes with a blessing to all saints in every place: **"The grace of our Lord Jesus Christ be with you all. Amen."**

What is it that John wants when he says that the grace of our Lord would be with us? His desire is that we would know the grace of this divine Person—the boundless, unfathomable, immutable divine grace of God Himself—not a temporary grace that does not keep His own, but a grace that will never allow His sheep to perish. It is the grace of our Lord Jesus Christ of whom it is written **"Having loved his own which were in the world, he loved them unto the end"** (John 13:1). It is the grace of which He said, **"No man is able to pluck them out of my father's hand"** (John 10:29). It is His saving grace that has everlastingly redeemed us from our sin and guilt.

And it is the grace of *our* Lord. Is this not a wonderful word? John's wish is that we may feel His tenderness, His brotherliness and His grace—because He is ours! He is my Savior and He is your Savior. An effectual ransom has been paid; He is our Redeemer. He has chosen, adopted, called, and sanctified us. May such grace be with us!

This benediction, the final words of Scripture, is John's most earnest prayer for believers. While the Old Testament ends with a curse, **"Lest I come and smite the earth with a curse"** (Malachi 4:6), the New Testament ends with a blessing, **"The grace of our Lord Jesus Christ be with you all. Amen."** This monumental blessing stands at the end of Revelation indicating what we have need of until He returns. Jesus said **"My grace is sufficient"** (2 Corinthians 12:9). By His grace, He will instruct us, cleanse us, enable us, strengthen us and transform us into His glorious image. His grace will be with us every hour, every day, in every way we may need it until He comes again. All we need between earth and heaven to fight against the devil, to overcome the world, and to enter into eternal joy is found in Christ.

"The grace of our Lord Jesus Christ be with you all. Amen."

125

Appendix

The Old Testament is filled with prophecies written over 2,500 years ago. Every one of these prophecies was fulfilled by Jesus Christ. Prophecies concerning the Second Coming of Jesus Christ remained unfulfilled, but the promise of Jesus is that they will be fulfilled in this generation.

Below is a list of some of the messianic Old Testament prophecies.

Genesis	Prophecy	Fulfillment
The Messiah would be born of the "seed" of a woman.	Genesis 3:15	Luke 1:34-35
The Messiah would defeat Satan.	above	1 John 3:8
The Messiah would suffer while reconciling men to God.	above	1 Peter 3:18
The Messiah would be a descendant of Shem.	Genesis 9:26	Luke 3:36
The Messiah would be a descendant of Abraham.	Genesis 12:3	Matthew 1:1
The Messiah would be a descendant of Isaac.	Genesis 17:19	Luke 3:34
The Messiah would be a descendant of Abraham.	Genesis 18:17-18	Matthew 1:1
The Messiah would come for all nations.	above	Acts 3:24-26
The Messiah would be a descendant of Isaac.	Genesis 21:12	Luke 3:34

The Messiah would be sacrificed on the same mountain where God tested Abraham.	Genesis 22:14	Luke 23:33
The Messiah would be a descendant of Abraham.	Genesis 22:18	Galatians 3:16
The Messiah would come for all nations.	above	Galatians 3:14
The Messiah would be a descendant of Isaac.	Genesis 26:4	Luke 3:34
The Messiah would be a descendant of Jacob.	Genesis 28:14	above
The Messiah would come for all people.	above	Galatians 3:26-29
The Messiah would be a descendant of Judah.	Genesis 49:10	Luke 3:33
The Messiah would be a King	above	John 1:49
The Jews' capitol punishment authority would be gone when the Messiah arrived.	above	John 18:31
Numbers		
The Messiah would be a King.	Numbers 24:17	John 19:19
Deuteronomy		
The Messiah would be a Prophet.	Deuteronomy 18:15-19	John 6:14
The Messiah would speak with words of authority given to Him from God.	above	John 12:48-50

Those who refused to listen to the Messiah would be judged.	above	above
The Messiah would be worshiped by angels at his birth.	Deuteronomy 32:43	Luke 2:13-14
Ruth		
The Messiah would be a descendant of Boaz & Ruth.	Ruth 4:12-17	Luke 3:32
1 Samuel		
The Messiah would be exalted by God with power and strength.	1 Samuel 2:10	Matthew 28:18
2 Samuel		
The Messiah would be a descendant of David.	2 Samuel 7:12-13	Matthew 1:1
The Messiah would be the Son of God.	above	Matthew 3:16-17
The Messiah would be a descendant of David.	2 Samuel 7:16	Matthew 1:1
The Messiah would come for all people.	2 Samuel 22:50	Romans 15:8-9
The Messiah would be the "Rock."	2 Samuel 23:2-4	1 Corinthians 10:4
The Messiah would be as the "light of the morning."	above	Revelation 22:16
1 Chronicles		
The Messiah would be a descendant of Judah.	1 Chronicles 5:2	Luke 3:33

The Messiah would be a descendant of David.	1 Chronicles 17:11-12	Luke 3:31
The Messiah's throne would be everlasting.	above	Luke 1:32-33
The Messiah would be the Son of God.	1 Chronicles 17:13-14	Matthew 3:16-17
Psalms		
The Messiah would be rejected by Gentiles.	Psalm 2:1	Acts 4:25-28
Political and religious leaders would conspire against the Messiah.	Psalm 2:2	Matthew 26:3-4
The Messiah would be a King.	Psalm 2:6	John 12:12-13
The Messiah would be the Son of God.	Psalm 2:7	Luke 1:31-35
The Messiah would declare that He was the Son of God.	above	John 9:35-37
The Messiah would be resurrected and crowned as King.	above	Acts 13:30-33
The Messiah would ask God for His inheritance.	Psalm 2:8	John 17:4-24
The Messiah would receive authority over all.	above	Matthew 28:18
The Messiah would be the Son of God.	Psalm 2:12	Matthew 17:5
The Messiah would reject those who did not believe in him.	above	John 3:36

Infants would give praise to the Messiah.	Psalm 8:2	Matthew 21:15-16
The Messiah would be given authority over all things.	Psalm 8:6	Matthew 28:18
The Messiah would be resurrected.	Psalm 16:8-10	Matthew 28:6
The Messiah's body would not be subject to decay.	above	Acts 13:35-37
The Messiah would be exalted to the presence of God.	Psalm 16:11	Acts 2:33
The Messiah would come for all people.	Psalm 18:49	Ephesians 3:4-6
The Messiah would cry out to God.	Psalm 22:1	Matthew 27:46
The Messiah would be forsaken by God.	above	Mark 15:34
The Messiah, anguished, would pray without ceasing.	Psalm 22:2	Matthew 26:38-39
The Messiah would be despised.	Psalm 22:6	Luke 23:21-23
The Messiah would be mocked by people shaking their heads.	Psalm 22:7	Matthew 27:39
Mockers would say of the Messiah, "He trusted God, let Him deliver him."	Psalm 22:8	Matthew 27:41-43
The Messiah would be aware of His Father from his youth.	Psalm 22:9	Luke 2:40

The Messiah would be called to God's service from the womb.	Psalm 22:10	Luke 1:30-33
The Messiah would be abandoned by the disciples.	Psalm 22:11	Mark 14:50
The Messiah would be surrounded by evil spirits.	Psalm 22:12-13	Colossians 2:15
The Messiah's heart would burst, flowing with blood & water.	Psalm 22:14	John 19:34
The Messiah would be crucified.	above	Matthew 27:35
The Messiah would thirst.	Psalm 22:15	John 19:28
The Messiah would thirst shortly before His death.	above	John 19:30
The Messiah would be surrounded by Gentiles at His crucifixion.	Psalm 22:16	Luke 23:36
The Messiah would be surrounded by Jews at His crucifixion.	above	Matthew 27:41-43
The Messiah's hands and feet would be pierced.	above	Matthew 27:38
None of the Messiah's bones would be broken.	Psalm 22:17	John 19:32-33
People would stare at the Messiah during His crucifixion.	above	Luke 23:35
The Messiah's garments would be divided.	Psalm 22:18	John 19:23-24
Lots would be cast for the Messiah's clothes.	above	above

The Messiah's atonement would enable believers to be his brethren.	Psalm 22:22	Hebrews 2:10-12
None of the Messiah's bones would be broken.	Psalm 34:20	John 19:32-33
The Messiah's offering of Himself would replace all sacrifices.	Psalm 40:6-8	Hebrews 10:10-13
The Messiah would say the scriptures were written of him.	above	Luke 24:44
The Messiah would come to do God's will.	Psalm 40:7-8	John 5:30
The Messiah would not conceal his mission from the congregation.	Psalm 40:9-10	Luke 4:16-21
The Messiah's betrayer would be a friend with whom He broke bread.	Psalm 41:9	Mark 14:17-18
The Messiah would speak with a message of grace.	Psalm 45:2	Luke 4:22
The Messiah's throne would be everlasting.	Psalm 45:6-7	Luke 1:31-33
The Messiah would be God.	above	Hebrews 1:8-9
The Messiah would act with righteousness.	above	John 5:30
The Messiah would ascend into heaven.	Psalm 68:18	Luke 24:51
The Messiah would give gifts to men.	above	Matthew 10:1
The Messiah would be hated by many without cause.	Psalm 69:4	Luke 23:13-22

The Messiah would bear reproach, for God's sake.	Psalm 69:7	Matthew 26:65-67
The Messiah would be rejected by the Jews.	Psalm 69:8	John 1:11
The Messiah's brothers would disbelieve Him.	above	John 7:3-5
The Messiah would be angered by disrespect toward the temple.	Psalm 69:9	John 2:13-17
The Messiah would bear reproach, for God's sake.	Psalm 69:9	Romans 15:3
The Messiah's disciples would fail Him in His time of need.	above	Mark 14:33-41
The Messiah would be offered gall and vinegar.	Psalm 69:21	Matthew 27:34
The Messiah would thirst.	above	John 19:28
The potter's field would be uninhabited.	Psalm 69:25	Acts 1:16-20
The Messiah would speak in parables.	Psalm 78:2	Matthew 13:34-35
The Messiah would be at the right hand of God.	Psalm 80:17	Acts 5:31
The Messiah would be a descendant of David.	Psalm 89:3-4	Matthew 1:1
The Messiah would call God His Father.	Psalm 89:26	Matthew 11:27
The Messiah would be God's "firstborn."	Psalm 89:27	Mark 16:6
The Messiah would be a descendant of David.	Psalm 89:29	Matthew 1:1
The Messiah would be a descendant of David.	Psalm 89:35-36	Matthew 1:1

The Messiah would be eternal.	Psalm 102:25-27	Colossians 1:17
The Messiah would be the creator of all.	above	John 1:3
The Messiah would be accused by false witnesses.	Psalm 109:2	John 18:29-30
The Messiah would pray for his enemies.	Psalm 109:4	Luke 23:34
The Messiah's betrayer would have a short life.	Psalm 109:8	Acts 1:16-18
The Messiah's betrayer would be replaced.	above	Acts 1:20-26
The Messiah would be mocked by people shaking their heads.	Psalm 109:25	Mark 15:29-30
The Messiah would be Lord.	Psalm 110:1	Matthew 22:41-45
The Messiah would be at the right hand of God.	above	Mark 16:19
The Messiah would be a Priest in the order of Melchizedek.	Psalm 110:4	Hebrews 6:17-20
The Messiah would be at the right hand of God.	Psalm 110:5	1 Peter 3:21-22
The Messiah would be the "stone" rejected by the Jews.	Psalm 118:22	Matthew 21:42-43
The Messiah would come in the name of the Lord.	Psalm 118:26	Matthew 21:9
The Messiah would be a descendant of David.	Psalm 132:11	Matthew 1:1
The Messiah would be a descendant of David.	Psalm 132:17	above

Proverbs		
The Messiah would be from everlasting.	Proverbs 8:22-23	John 17:5
The Messiah would ascend and descend from heaven.	Proverbs 30:4	John 3:13
God would have a Son.	above	Matthew 3:16-17
Isaiah		
The Jews would have a hardened heart against the Messiah.	Isaiah 6:9-10	John 12:37-40
The Messiah would speak in parables.	Isaiah 6:9-10	Matthew 13:13-15
The Messiah would be a descendant of David.	Isaiah 7:13-14	Matthew 1:1
The Messiah would be born of a virgin.	Isaiah 7:14	Luke 1:34-35
The Messiah would be Immanuel, "God with us."	above	Matthew 1:21-23
The Messiah would be God.	above	John 12:45
The Messiah would be a "stumbling stone" for the Jews.	Isaiah 8:14	Matthew 21:43-44
The Messiah would minister in Galilee.	Isaiah 9:1-2	Matthew 4:12-17
The Messiah would be a light to the Gentiles.	above	Luke 2:28-32
The birth of the Messiah.	Isaiah 9:6	Luke 2:11
The Messiah would be the Son of God.	above	Luke 1:35

The Messiah would be the "Wonderful Counselor."	above	John 7:46
The Messiah would be both God and man (the "Mighty God").	above	John 10:30
The Messiah would be from everlasting (the "Everlasting Father").	above	Revelation 1:8
The Messiah would be the "Prince of Peace."	above	Colossians 1:20
The Messiah would be a descendant of David.	Isaiah 9:7	Matthew 1:1
The Messiah would be a descendant of Jesse.	Isaiah 11:1	Luke 3:23-32
The Messiah would grow up in a poor family.	above	Luke 2:7
The Messiah would have the full Spirit of God upon Him.	Isaiah 11:2	Matthew 3:16-17
The Messiah would have the Spirit of Wisdom.	above	Luke 2:40
The Messiah would have the Spirit of Understanding.	above	above
The Messiah would have the Spirit of Counsel.	above	Matthew 7:28-29
The Messiah would have the Spirit of Might.	above	Matthew 8:27
The Messiah would have the Spirit of the Knowledge of God.	above	John 7:29
The Messiah would have the Spirit of the Fear of God.	above	Hebrews 5:7

The Messiah would have a quick understanding in the fear of the Lord.	Isaiah 11:3	Luke 2:46-47
The Messiah would not judge on the basis of external representations.	above	John 7:24
The Messiah would judge the poor with righteousness.	Isaiah 11:4	Mark 12:41-44
The Messiah would be a descendant of Jesse.	Isaiah 11:10	Luke 3:23-32
The Messiah would come for all people.	above	Acts 13:47-48
The Messiah would have the key of David.	Isaiah 22:22	Revelation 3:7
The Messiah would defeat death.	Isaiah 25:8	Revelation 1:18
Others would rise to life at the resurrection of the Messiah.	Isaiah 26:19	Matthew 27:52-53
The Messiah would be the cornerstone.	Isaiah 28:16	1 Peter 2:4-6
The Messiah would heal the blind.	Isaiah 35:5	Mark 10:51-52
The Messiah would heal the deaf.	above	Mark 7:32-35
The Messiah would heal the lame.	Isaiah 35:6	Matthew 12:10-13
The Messiah would heal the dumb.	above	Matthew 9:32-33
The forerunner of the Messiah would live in the wilderness.	Isaiah 40:3	Matthew 3:1-4

The forerunner would prepare people for the coming of the Messiah.	above	Luke 1:17
The Messiah would be God.	above	John 10:30
The Messiah would be as a shepherd.	Isaiah 40:11	John 10:11
The Messiah would be God's servant.	Isaiah 42:1	John 4:34
The Messiah would have the Spirit of God upon Him.	above	Matthew 3:16-17
The Messiah would please God.	above	Matthew 3:16-17
The Messiah would provide "justice" to the Gentiles.	above	Matthew 24:14
The Messiah would not draw attention to Himself.	Isaiah 42:2	Matthew 12:15
The Messiah would have compassion for the poor and needy.	Isaiah 42:3	Matthew 11:4-5
The Messiah would receive guidance from God.	Isaiah 42:6	John 5:19-20
The Messiah would be ministered to by God.	above	John 8:29
The Messiah would be the new covenant.	above	Matthew 26:28
The Messiah would be a light to the Gentiles.	above	John 8:12
The Messiah would heal the blind.	Isaiah 42:7	Matthew 9:27-30
The Messiah would be from everlasting.	Isaiah 48:16	John 1:1-2

The Messiah would be sent from God.	above	John 7:29
The Messiah would come for all people.	Isaiah 49:1	1 Timothy 2:4-6
The Messiah would be called to God's service from the womb.	above	Matthew 1:20-21
The Messiah would be called by His name before He was born.	above	Luke 1:30-31
The Messiah's words would be as a sharp sword.	Isaiah 49:2	Revelation 2:12-16
The Messiah would be protected by God.	above	Matthew 2:13-15
The Messiah would be responsible for the judgment of mankind.	above	John 5:22-29
The Messiah would be God's servant.	Isaiah 49:3	John 17:4
The Messiah's work would glorify God.	above	Matthew 15:30-31
The Messiah would be distressed over the Jews' unbelief.	Isaiah 49:4	Luke 19:41-42
The Messiah would be rejected by the Jews.	above	John 5:43
The Messiah would be God's servant.	Isaiah 49:5	John 6:38
The Messiah would come to bring Israel back to God.	above	Matthew 15:24
The Messiah would be God's servant.	Isaiah 49:6	John 12:49-50

The Messiah would be a light to the Gentiles.	above	Acts 13:47-48
The Messiah would be despised.	Isaiah 49:7	John 10:20
The Messiah would speak with knowledge given to Him from God.	Isaiah 50:4	John 12:49
The Messiah would not be rebellious to God's will.	Isaiah 50:5	John 12:27
The Messiah's back would be whipped.	Isaiah 50:6	Matthew 27:26
The Messiah's face would be beaten and spit upon.	above	Matthew 26:67
The Messiah would steadfastly set His face toward His mission.	Isaiah 50:7	Luke 9:51-53
The Messiah would be justified by His righteousness.	Isaiah 50:8	1 Timothy 3:16
The Messiah would place His trust in God.	Isaiah 50:8-10	John 11:7-10
The Messiah would be God's servant.	Isaiah 52:13	John 9:4
The Messiah would be highly exalted.	above	Philippians 2:9-11
The Messiah's face would be disfigured from severe beatings.	Isaiah 52:14	Matthew 26:67-68
The Messiahs blood would be shed to make atonement for all.	Isaiah 52:15	Revelation 1:5
The Messiah's own people would not believe He was the Christ.	Isaiah 53:1	John 12:37-38

The Messiah would grow up in a poor family.	Isaiah 53:2	Luke 2:7
The Messiah would have the appearance of an ordinary man.	above	Philippians 2:7-8
The Messiah would be despised.	Isaiah 53:3	Luke 4:28-29
The Messiah would be rejected.	above	Matthew 27:21-23
The Messiah would have great sorrow and grief.	above	Luke 19:41-42
Men would hide from being associated with the Messiah.	above	Mark 14:50-52
The Messiah would have a healing ministry.	Isaiah 53:4	Luke 6:17-19
The Messiah would bear and carry upon himself the sins of the world.	above	1 Peter 2:24
The Messiah would be thought to be cursed by God.	above	Matthew 27:41-43
The Messiah would bear the penalty for mankind's transgressions.	Isaiah 53:5	Luke 23:33
The Messiah's sacrifice would provide peace between man and God.	above	Colossians 1:20
The Messiah's back would be whipped.	Isaiah 53:5	Matthew 27:26
The Messiah would be the sin-bearer for all mankind.	Isaiah 53:6	Galatians 1:4

It was God's will that the Messiah would be the sin-bearer for all mankind.	above	1 John 4:10
The Messiah would be oppressed and afflicted.	Isaiah 53:7	Matthew 27:27-31
The Messiah would be silent before His accusers.	above	Matthew 27:12-14
The Messiah would be as a sacrificial lamb.	above	John 1:29
The Messiah would be confined and persecuted.	Isaiah 53:8	Matthew 26:55
The Messiah would be judged.	above	John 18:13-22
The Messiah would be killed.	above	Matthew 27:35
The Messiah would die for the sins of the world.	above	1 John 2:2
The Messiah would be buried in a rich man's grave.	Isaiah 53:9	Matthew 27:57
The Messiah would be innocent and have done no violence.	above	Mark 15:3
The Messiah would have no deceit in his mouth.	above	John 18:38
It was God's will that the Messiah would die for all mankind.	Isaiah 53:10	John 18:11
The Messiah would be an offering for sin.	above	Matthew 20:28
The Messiah would be resurrected and live forever.	above	Mark 16:16

The Messiah would prosper.	above	John 17:1-5
God would be fully satisfied with the suffering of the Messiah.	Isaiah 53:11	John 12:27
The Messiah would be God's servant.	above	Romans 5:18-19
The Messiah would justify man before God.	above	Romans 5:8-9
The Messiah would be the sin-bearer for all mankind.	above	Hebrews 9:28
Because of His sacrifice, the Messiah would be greatly exalted by God.	Isaiah 53:12	Matthew 28:18
The Messiah would give up His life to save mankind.	above	Luke 23:46
The Messiah would be grouped with criminals.	above	Luke 23:32
The Messiah would be the sin-bearer for all mankind.	above	2 Corinthians 5:21
The Messiah would intercede with God on behalf of mankind.	above	Luke 23:34
The Messiah would be resurrected by God.	Isaiah 55:3	Acts 13:34
The Messiah would be a witness.	Isaiah 55:4	John 18:37
The Messiah would come to provide salvation.	Isaiah 59:15-16	John 6:40
The Messiah would be the intercessor between man and God.	above	Matthew 10:32-33
The Messiah would come to Zion as their Redeemer.	Isaiah 59:20	Luke 2:38

The Messiah would have the Spirit of God upon Him.	Isaiah 61:1-2	Matthew 3:16-17
The Messiah would preach the good news.	above	Luke 4:17-21
The Messiah would provide freedom from the bondage of sin and death.	above	John 8:31-32
The Messiah would proclaim a period of grace.	above	John 5:24
Jeremiah		
The Messiah would be a descendant of David.	Jeremiah 23:5-6	Luke 3:23-31
The Messiah would be God.	above	John 13:13
The Messiah would be both man and God.	above	1 Timothy 3:16
The Messiah would be born of a virgin.	Jeremiah 31:22	Matthew 1:18-20
The Messiah would be the new covenant.	Jeremiah 31:31	Matthew 26:28
The Messiah would be a descendant of David.	Jeremiah 33:14-15	Luke 3:23-31
Ezekiel		
The Messiah would be a descendant of David.	Ezekiel 17:22-24	Luke 3:31
The Messiah would be a descendant of David.	Ezekiel 34:23-24	Matthew 1:1
Daniel		
The Messiah would ascend into heaven.	Daniel 7:13-14	Acts 1:9-11

The Messiah would be highly exalted.	above	Ephesians 1:20-22
The Messiah's dominion would be everlasting.	above	Luke 1:31-33
The Messiah would come to make an end to sins.	Daniel 9:24	Galatians 1:3-5
The Messiah would be holy.	above	Luke 1:35
The Messiah would enter Jerusalem 483 years, after the decree to rebuild Jerusalem.	Daniel 9:25	John 12:12-13
The Messiah would be killed.	Daniel 9:26	Matthew 27:35
The Messiah would die for the sins of the world.	above	Hebrews 2:9
The Messiah would be killed before the destruction of the temple.	above	Matthew 27:50-51
A vision of the Messiah in a glorified state.	Daniel 10:5-6	Revelation 1:13-16
Hosea		
The Messiah would defeat death.	Hosea 13:14	1 Corinthians 15:55-57
Joel		
The Messiah would offer salvation to all mankind.	Joel 2:32	Romans 10:12-13
Micah		
The Messiah would be born in Bethlehem.	Micah 5:2	Matthew 2:1-2

The Messiah would be God's servant.	above	John 15:10
The Messiah would be from everlasting.	above	Revelation 1:8
Haggai		
The Messiah would visit the second temple.	Haggai 2:6-9	Luke 2:27
The Messiah would be a descendant of Zerubbabel.	Haggai 2:23	Luke 3:27
Zechariah		
The Messiah would be God's servant.	Zechariah 3:8	John 17:4
The Messiah would be Priest and King.	Zechariah 6:12-13	Hebrews 8:1
The Messiah would be greeted with rejoicing in Jerusalem.	Zechariah 9:9	Matthew 21:8-10
The Messiah would be beheld as King.	above	John 12:12-13
The Messiah would be just.	above	John 5:30
The Messiah would bring salvation.	above	Luke 19:10
The Messiah would be humble.	above	Matthew 11:29
The Messiah would be presented to Jerusalem riding on a donkey.	above	Matthew 21:6-9
The Messiah would be the cornerstone.	Zechariah 10:4	Ephesians 2:20
At the time of Messiah's coming, Israel would have unfit leaders.	Zechariah 11:4-6	Matthew 23:1-4

The Messiah's rejection would cause God to remove His protection of Israel.	above	Luke 19:41-44
The Messiah would be rejected in favor of another king.	above	John 19:13-15
The Messiah would have a ministry to the "poor," the believing remnant.	Zechariah 11:7	Matthew 9:35-36
The unbelief of Israel's leaders would force the Messiah to reject them.	Zechariah 11:8	Matthew 23:33
The Messiah would be despised.	above	Matthew 27:20
The Messiah would stop ministering to the those who rejected Him.	Zechariah 11:9	Matthew 13:10-11
The Messiah's rejection would cause God to remove His protection of Israel.	Zechariah 11:10-11	Luke 19:41-44
The Messiah would be God.	above	John 14:7
The Messiah would be betrayed for thirty pieces of silver.	Zechariah 11:12-13	Mathew 26:14-15
The Messiah would be rejected.	above	above
Thirty pieces of silver would be thrown into the house of the Lord.	above	Matthew 27:3-5
The Messiah would be God.	above	John 12:45

The Messiah's body would be pierced.	Zechariah 12:10	John 19:34-37
The Messiah would be both God and man.	above	John 10:30
The Messiah would be rejected.	above	John 1:11
It was God's will that the Messiah would die for all mankind.	Zechariah 13:7	John 18:11
The Messiah would die a violent death.	above	Matthew 27:35
The Messiah would be both God and man.	above	John 14:9
Israel would be scattered as a result of rejecting the Messiah	above	Matthew 26:31
Malachi		
A messenger would prepare the way for the Messiah.	Malachi 3:1	Matthew 11:10
The Messiah would make a sudden appearance at the temple.	above	Mark 11:15-16
The Messiah would be the messenger of the new covenant.	above	Luke 4:43
The Messiah's forerunner would come in the spirit of Elijah.	Malachi 4:5	Matthew 3:1-2
The Messiah's forerunner would turn many to righteousness.	Malachi 4:6	Luke 1:16-17 [56]

[56] http://www.preservedwords.com/prophecies.html